Software Defined-WAN for the Digital Age

Software Defined-WAN for the Digital Age

A Bold Transition to Next Generation Networking

David W. Wang

CRC Press
Taylor & Francis Group
Boca Raton London New York

CRC Press is an imprint of the
Taylor & Francis Group, an **informa** business

CRC Press
Taylor & Francis Group
6000 Broken Sound Parkway NW, Suite 300
Boca Raton, FL 33487-2742

First issued in paperback 2020

ISBN 13: 978-0-367-57083-5 (pbk)
ISBN 13: 978-1-138-34599-7 (hbk)

Visit the Taylor & Francis Web site at
http://www.taylorandfrancis.com

and the CRC Press Web site at
http://www.crcpress.com

Contents

Preface: Debut a New WAN

The SD-WAN arena is very dynamic and fast evolving. According to the original plan of this publishing, a gentleman who leads a boutique consulting firm based in Silicon Valley enabling and supporting VeloCloud Networks, Inc.* in SD-WAN marketing campaigns would write up a Foreword for this new book of mine. However, by December 2017, VMWare acquired VeloCloud and this move also brought some unexpected impacts and changes to firms who used to partner with VeloCloud, as well as the tentative Foreword writer for this book.

Thus, we switch to Plan B: it should be a good idea to present this Preface with some recent C-level public quotations from several major service providers as they launch their SD-WAN services, because these executive remarks represent well the industry's conceptual and strategic thinking on SD-WAN and its trend.

Here we go:

> "As the equipment vendors have improved the efficiency of their processors, allowing encryption to occur in a multipath format through the processor instead of serially we're seeing that efficiency go from like 40 or 50% to the 80% … As that occurs, SD-WAN will become the

* A "pure play" SD-WAN technology and service firm founded in 2012 and has now been acquired by VMWare.

dominant platform for location-to-location private networking and will replace MPLS."

*Dave Schaeffer, CEO of Cogent, during the 2018 Global TMT West Conference** *Jan 9–11, 2018*

"The WAN is one of the most critical components of any enterprise network infrastructure and can be complex and challenging to manage ... Zayo's SD-WAN makes WAN management easier and more efficient, providing better performance, flexibility and reliability."

Mike Strople, president of Zayo Enterprise Networks† *Jan 3, 2018*

"We invest all our efforts in giving customers choice, security, resilience, service, and agility in the roll out of high performance networks that support their digital transformation—what we call Dynamic Network Services.

"This announcement is an important stage in the acceleration of that investment. Agile Connect gives BT customers a very robust SD-WAN at the right price, designed with ease of use and customer experience at its heart. It combines the technology of world-class partners and our own expertise in SDN with our global network and Cloud services capabilities to bring more control, flexibility, performance and security for our customers."

Maria Grazia Pecorari, President, Digital, Global Portfolio & Marketing, Global Services, BT‡ *Sept 27, 2017*

"Today we are delighted to offer a new industry benchmark in enterprise network services for the new business world ... CTG's industry experience, along with the strengths of China Telecom, enables a fast, seamless, secure and on-the-go experience for our customers. SD-WAN is the future for businesses—especially SMEs—seeking greater access,

* Fiercetelecom.com Jan 12, 2018.

† Zayo.com. Jan 3, 2018.

‡ Globaltelecombusiness.com. Sept 27, 2017.

capacity, speed and control. Together with Versa Networks, we are committed to the evolution of SD-WAN."

*Joe Han, Executive Vice President, China Telecom Global** *Sept 15, 2017*

"Business is moving at an unprecedented pace and, in an effort to remain relevant, organizations have deployed technologies from multiple providers. With real-time insights into how network components are working together and performing, CIOs, network architects and developers are empowered with information shaping existing and future IT strategies."

Enzo Cocotti, director at Optus Business† *Sept 14, 2017*

"The rapid change in technology is driving companies to consider SD-WAN as the answer to simplifying network challenges … The SD-WAN dashboard provides our customers with real-time, detailed visibility into the performance of their entire WAN and all of their applications, while single-click deployment minimizes the set-up time for branch offices and temporary sites."

Mike Fitz, VP of the Global Wireline Business Unit at Sprint‡ *May 16, 2017*

"Today's dynamic information technology environment requires enterprises to be more agile as they expand operations, introduce new applications and migrate to public Clouds—all while continuously optimizing costs … These factors are driving the need for more intelligent use of broadband Internet connectivity in global hybrid network architectures."

Tim Naramore, CTO, Masergy§ *Sept. 13, 2016*

"We really had to ask ourselves how we were going to handle branch office solutions beyond transport, how we were going to move beyond Layer-2 to get into branch office networking and application

* Marketwired.com. Sept 15, 2017.
† CIO.com.au. Sept 14, 2017.
‡ Sprint.com. May 16 2017.
§ Masergy.com. Sept 13, 2016.

prioritization and all the things that have been handled by MPLS … We have never had to apologize for TDM or T1s and we could always talk about broadband, hosted voice or whatever the lean-forward answer was, and the lean-forward answer is SD-WAN."

Kevin O'Toole, SVP of product management for Comcast Business May 16, 2017*

* Fiercetelecom.com. May 16, 2017.

Acknowledgments

Special thanks to Richard O'Hanley—Publisher—ICT and Security, Todd Perry—Project Editor, and Jonathan Pennell from CRC Press/ Taylor & Francis Group; Emeline Jarvie—Associate Project Manager from codemantra; and Hyden and Susan from my family for their professional work and strong support during the process of this book's publication.

Introduction: SD-WAN—A Game Changer for Network Solutions

When Cloud Computing as a solution and service was debuting about 7 or 8 years ago, I was amazed by its core technologies such as virtualization, VM abstraction, and centralized software control, as well as the disruptive impact and changes that Cloud has brought about to the industry and market. (For more details, please refer to my book *Cash in on Cloud Computing* published in March 2015.)

One puzzle, however, is that as a seasoned telecommunication and network professional, I see that Cloud computing is tilted more towards a revolution for either on premise or data center-based enterprise IT operations, which have become more agile, responsive, and cost effective. Yet the traditional wide area network (WAN) model based on dedicated connection and proprietary hardware has mostly remained costly, complex, and inefficient.

What changes can be made to the networking sector? What innovations can make WAN, which plays a vital integrated part of the Cloud ecosystem, more cost effective, performance robust, provisioning efficient, service secure, and operation intelligent?

This is what this new book of mine cares about, and Software Defined (SD)-WAN is the answer. (Note: The assumption is that readers of this book already possess some basic knowledge about data networking, WAN telecommunications, IT operations, and Cloud computing.)

For the enterprise market over the past 15 years or so, distributed broadband network services primarily include the private IP Multiprotocol Label Switching (MPLS) and public broadband Internet. Both have pros and cons. For instance, while MPLS is reliable, guaranteed in class of services, and secured, it is quite costly and slow in upgrading or adding new sites.

Also, traditional WAN like MPLS is not designed for directly connecting an enterprise office to Cloud-powered applications such as Office 365 or Salesforce.com or Cloud-hosted Unified Communications. The public Internet, on the other hand, while it can offset many cons of the MPLS, is less manageable in terms of quality, reliability, and security.

Nowadays major business applications from Cloud, mobile, big data, and Internet of Things traffic put increased strain on the legacy WAN infrastructure and call for a new WAN. Apparently, it would be great to have a next-gen type of WAN solution that absorbs the pros from both MPLS and public Internet while minimizing their cons.

This is exactly why SD-WAN has come into play. Conceptually, one can simply deem SD-WAN as an optimized combination of MPLS and public Internet in characteristics and features. Software Defined Networking (SDN) and Network Function Virtualization (NFV) are the core technologies of SD-WAN, which enable SD-WAN to become more intelligent and cost saving than ever before in its operation and performance.

SD-WAN is an advanced networking approach that creates hybrid networks to integrate broadband or other network services into the corporate WAN, not only just handling general business workloads and traffic, but also being capable of maintaining the performance and security of real-time and sensitive applications. SD-WAN also makes a new digital platform to host and enable more innovative enterprise applications.

No wonder SD-WAN is quickly catching the industry and market's attention and massive implementations are already underway from both enterprises and services providers. A 2016 survey of enterprise communications professionals found that 30% of respondents plan to migrate to SD-WAN within 1–2 years.*

---

* Network World from IDG, August 1, 2017.

Based on some recent research by Cisco Systems, SD-WAN will account for 25% of IP WAN traffic by 2021, up from 6% in 2016. Traditional WAN traffic growth will slow down to approximately 5% and gradually to a halt.* According to IDC's Worldwide SD-WAN Forecast, over the next 5 years, 2017–2021, SD-WAN sales will grow at a 69% compound annual growth rate, hitting $8.05 billion in 2021.†

While traditional router vendors, such as Cisco and Juniper and established WAN optimization vendors such as Riverbed Technology, Silver Peak, Aryaka, and Citrix will all play in the new SD-WAN market, the so called "pure play" SD-WAN startups such as VeloCloud (now bought over by VMware), Viptela (now acquired by Cisco), CloudGenix, Versa, and Talari are taking a lot of limelight on this brand new platform.

These vendors are teaming up with major communication service providers (CSPs) and Cloud providers like AT&T, Verizon, CenturyLink, BT, Orange, Deutsche Telekom, NTT, China Telecom Global, etc., in rolling out SD-WAN domestically and globally.

Hence the technology, solution, market, business drivers, and key players for SD-WAN are all here. The challenges become how the enterprise can effectively adopt SD-WAN so as to "pay less to do more" in WAN networking and how the CSPs can quickly take SD-WAN to market as a niche of their service portfolio, realizing new revenue streams, growing market shares, and improving customer satisfaction. In a nutshell, how can we cash in on SD-WAN in this new digital era and transcend the WAN market to the next level?

This book tries to address these challenges and let's kick off the exciting tour. The book processes three chapters covering SD-WAN from the perspectives of technology evolution, enterprise adoption, and service provider portfolio & Go to Market. With some quite fresh use cases and insightful dialogues included, the book tends to

---

* Cisco Visual Networking Index™ (VNI) Complete Forecast released on June 8, 2017.

† IDC Worldwide SD-WAN Forecast, 2017–2021 released on July 27, 2017.

provide the readers with some easy-to-follow and inspiring insights on next-gen network solutions and services.

David W. Wang
Managing Principal
ITCom Global, LLC
September 2018

1

Highlights of SD-WAN Evolution

A Conversation with an SD-WAN Evangelist

> Software-defined wide-area network (SD-WAN) for the first time turns the network functions into an intelligent ecosystem.

At the end of 2017, I got a chance to have an insightful conversation with an SD-WAN solution evangelist and we talked about SD-WAN's start-off, status quo, and future trends.

Author (A): I've heard you are a strong advocate of SD-WAN in terms of technologies and services.

Evangelist (E): Yes, that's right. I've spent past 5 years introducing and promoting SD-WAN sometimes as an alternative, sometimes a supplement to the legacy WAN solutions, with MPLS in particular.

A: What exactly the amazing changes do you see from SD-WAN? What's new in it?

E: Well, the biggest change is that SD-WAN is making WAN smarter and agile from the network function perspective, and less costly with shorter installation time from the business operation perspective. An analogy would be that the network used to function just like a machine, or it's made of many pieces of machines like routers, switches, gateway, fire walls, CPEs (customer-premise equipment), and accelerators along the network. Are they controllable and operational? Yes, but often in a difficult, slow, and less effective way, because imagine when you have these so many machines and devices to manage.

A: So, SD-WAN is not functioning like a machine anymore?

E: Not like an old-style machine. I would say SD-WAN for the first time turns the network functions into an intelligent ecosystem. For example, human being is an intelligent ecosystem, our heart pumps blood and maintains the life, while our brain controls thinking and manages the actions, in a central manner. Our body obtains energies from the heart and follows the right instructions from the brain.

A: How is this like the way SD-WAN works?

E: Now advanced software and virtualization technologies (called SDN and NFV) allow us to simplify the hardware devices like routers and firewalls, decouple the data plane and control plane of routers, and manage the network from a central orchestration point with great scalability. The result is network becomes more organic (vs. mechanic), automatic (vs. manual), and responsive (vs. numb) in its performance and management. SD-WAN now makes the so-called edge network possible, which better serves the end users.

A: That sounds very exciting. Still some folks think SD-WAN as just another buzzword and its service has no significant difference with like such existing solutions as network optimization.

E: Such notion is incorrect. Network optimization's goal is to make the most effective use possible of the limited bandwidth available across the WAN link by applying several techniques like deduplication, compression, reduced latency, and caching to name a few. SD-WAN on the other hand, specializes in real-time network scenarios, accounting for jitter, latency, and packet loss to ensure that traffic is traveling optimally across the WAN along the best routes.

A: Can these two services work together?

E: Yes. Some SD-WAM offers include the optimization feature, and some offers makes it optional if the clients have missional critical and real time traffic to send through. The difference is SD-WAN allows more control over the holistic network operations instead of just a single route.

A: OK, very helpful. Another puzzle people have is that often SD-WAN will run an overlay on top of public Internet service. Hence is SD-WAN reliable enough for enterprise class of communications?

E: I would say SD-WAN is reliable in most cases for two key reasons. First, its central orchestration, control, and intelligent routing would allow traffic to go through the best routes of the Internet and reach the destination as a private network like MPLS can handle. Second, the fast growing all fiber network infrastructure and enhanced Internet technologies as being deployed in most of developed regions and countries will help to make the quality, availability, and performance of public Internet close to the private IP network.

A: Then what's its difference with the IPsec VPN that we are already familiar with?

E: Good question. As for IPsec VPN, the tunnel, encryption, and overlay idea are pretty similar to SD-WAN. But IPsec VPN is just a secured tunnel without much traffic management mechanism, while SD-WAN offers much more and takes care of lots of network complexity with building redundant tunnels, monitoring the quality of the tunnels and failing over.

A: How has SD-WAN been doing in the market?

E: I would say 2012–2013 was about the SD-WAN concept kickoff; 2014–2015 was initial productization and technology polishing up. 2016–2018 is about rolling out the service offer both from technology vendors and telecom service providers. The adoption is really heating up.

A: What's your prediction for SD-WAN in the next 3–5 years?

E: SD-WAN solution will take off and come as a new normal for WAN solutions. I don't see SD-WAN will completely replace MPLS, rather it will work as a supplementary alternative in some cases especially for regional and long-haul traffic. This is like you take an airline to a destination, you would have economy, economy plus, business, and first-class seating choices. Some business mission critical data may still be better off routing over MPLS, while other traffic will be fine riding on SD-WAN. Anyway, enterprises now have more options for their WAN services.

A: From this sense, do you still see SD-WAN disruptive enough as a next-gen network solution?

E: Of course. Some companies may prefer MPLS+SD-WAN hybrid, while others may totally de-plug MPLS and just use

SD-WAN over the public Internet. Overall SD-WAN will significantly lower the WAN service cost, enhance agility, performance, and security, plus directly linking business to the Cloud in high speed. Although it may not completely take over MPLS, 65%–75% taking away of legacy MPLS traffic is very possible. By doing so it would become quite disruptive in the WAN service evolution.

A: So, can we say SD-WAN will be a new network solution most enterprises can't do without from now on?

E: Yes, we can. I would prefer to call it a new "digital platform."

Call for a New WAN of the Digital Age

The Fourth Industrial Revolution or Industry Revolution 4.0 is underway, and it is a name for the current trend of automation and data exchange in manufacturing and IT technologies. It's agreed that this new revolution, as illustrated in Figure 1.1, will be marked by such advanced technologies as artificial intelligence (AI), robots including unmanned vehicles, digital transformation and ecosystem like smart Cloud computing, big data, Internet of Things (IoT), 5th Generation (5G) cellular, etc.

Digital transformation is the ability to orchestrate apps, networks, and devices to provide seamless access to digital services for end users, where the network is the foundation of any digital transformation effort, because network is the one thing that connects everything.

Figure 1.1 The fourth industrial revolution.

The next-gen wide-area network (WAN) that connects local area networks (LANs) together over geographic areas must evolve to support digital transformation. The next-gen WAN includes both wireline and wireless, in the form of all fiber optic data networks, as well as 5G wireless technology and solutions.

Today many large enterprises have started to establish digital transformation initiatives and task teams to drive their innovations and decision-making. Leading initiatives include AI/machine learning, IoT, hybrid Cloud architecture, and the SD-WAN that this book intends to cover. All these are shaping the next-gen IT and networking ecosystem.

Cloud Apps and Smart Networking as Drivers

Now new applications in the nature of digital transformation are taking over as major WAN bandwidth consumptions.

Today, as a result of digital transformation, the WAN is responsible for carrying a wide array of traffic for many applications for streamlined collaboration and communication within an organization and across organizations. Also, Cloud-based IT operations have changed the way data traffic moves and the location where these applications are hosted.

In the past, corporate voice, data sharing, web activities, and video conference made the mainstream of WAN traffic. Now, new applications in the nature of digital transformation are taking over as major WAN bandwidth consumptions.

According to Enterprise Management Associates (EMA) research, big data traffic now tops the list of applications that consume the most WAN bandwidth, about 30% of the overall network traffic. Storage backups/restores consumption comes the second as 28%. Cloud-native applications and external Cloud applications were each cited as the top consumer by 24% of respondents, placing them third on the list of top bandwidth hogs.*

* EMA Report: Digital Transformation Demands a Next-Generation Wide-Area Network released in December 2016.

The Cloud-based applications that are essential for modern businesses have drastically different traffic patterns and volumes compared to traditional on-premises applications and require high-bandwidth and low-latency connections, calling for a robust new WAN for the digital age, with the following key characteristics:

Handling Cloud-Centric Traffic

Today's Cloud-centric traffic flow in general includes Cloud-based application like Office 365 and Gmail, mobile data and videos, big data analytics, and Cloud-hosted solutions like a virtual call center. But the existing enterprise WAN is a highly centralized, controlled, and self-contained IT environment with static hardware-based networking. It is neither designed to handle such Cloud-centric traffic nor cost prohibitive in handling such traffic.

Effective Cloud operations would depend on a robust and reliable network in place between the Cloud and end users and the next-gen WAN must become a more distributed, fragmented, and dynamic ecosystem.

Smart Routing and Security Capability

The new WAN should get smarter with such strong capabilities like allowing intelligent and application-based routing, network optimization, active load balancing, latency and packet-loss conditioning, blackout and brownout detection, fast session or packet level failover, and security real-time monitoring, isolating, and resolving. Only software based central control with the hardware disaggregation will make such advanced capabilities possible.

Cost Reduction for Both Service Providers and Enterprise Users

The new WAN should help businesses reduce cost in two ways: service cost and opportunity cost. Provided as a fully managed service globally, the new WAN should ensure enterprises save on subscription cost, and the solutions delivered through network overlay, virtualization, and the Cloud should help reduce capital expenditures. That is, on-premises infrastructure is no longer required to launch the new WAN model.

The new WAN meanwhile ensures the service providers save network maintenance and management costs and improves uptime with the threats and potential costs of downtime reduced. In this way it enables enterprise and service providers IT resources to be free of network routine work and focus on more strategic business initiatives.

Agility in Deployment and Provisioning

Legacy network technologies like Multiprotocol Label Switching (MPLS) are very inflexible, and often deploying a new site or location can take 60–120 days, negatively impacting business expansion and productivity. In contrast, the market expects the new WAN deployment can be initialized in days and upgraded or changed in hours. For CPE deployment, virtual CPE (vCPE) with thin and plug-and-play DIY (do it yourself) capabilities are preferred over the traditional CPE box that required technicians on site for installation, testing, and launch.

Branch Office Optimization

The trend is that most enterprises are switching away from centralized network architectures (mostly in the sense of hardware constrained topology, and not to be confused with the SD-WAN central control/orchestration empowered by SDN), and instead allowing remote sites to connect directly to public Cloud services. Centralized network often slows down and interferes with smooth Cloud access. Hence, most mission-critical applications should be accessed through the Cloud, with simplified network operations at disparate branches. The branches will not (or as little as possible) host devices on-premises, minimizing the need for on-site hardware management and maintenance.

Handling Internet of Things Traffic

IoT device growth means we see more remote network connections to machines and devices. From the networking standpoint, IoT traffic requires new bandwidth pattern, new security controls, new Quality of Service (QoS) polices, and much more.

Organizational function wise, IoT also often means disconnect between business and IT, because while IT means information technology, IoT mostly is about operation technology and is managed by the Operation Department of an enterprise. Hence, enterprises would need a new WAN solution to bridge the gap between business and IT and it must be an easy-to-comprehend and converge technology.

A Couple of Use Cases in the New Front

In one use case, Company A now must consider the traffic needs and management of different types of Cloud-based applications, how that traffic is routed across a WAN, and how to get the most value to meet organizational objectives. Any traffic that carries the company's Unified Communications as a Service (UCaaS) is generally more important than traffic from social media sites like Facebook or YouTube. Besides prioritization, user experience, QoS, and service level agreements (SLAs) are important factors to keep in mind as well. The bottom line: the Cloud-based IT operations should not differ greatly with on-premises IT operations, and the Cloud connectivity plays a vital role in this process.

In another case for Company B, for cost-saving purposes, they can send certain types of application traffic to specific routing paths, provided other traffic can be routed along different paths. Some paths must also meet the SLA while others can be on "best effort" basis. This can be done via a hybrid network structure. WAN routing protocols may dictate that voice traffic can be routed via the MPLS connection with a lower bandwidth and higher SLA with lower latency and drop rate, whereas their data traffic is routed via high-bandwidth broadband Internet or some other new breed of WAN solution.

SD-WAN Is Born

With all the driving forces described above, a new WAN is born.

We call it SD-WAN—an innovative approach to WAN networking based on organic and flexible software control; intelligent, virtualized, and responsive edge technologies; policy automation and real-time orchestration of all components of connectivity and access; and agnostic to underlay network infrastructure. It is used to connect enterprise networks—including branch offices and data centers—across large and long geographic distances.

In other words, SD-WAN is an ecosystem of thin hardware including vCPEs or edge devices, robust software including controllers, and innovative features that enables enterprise-grade WAN performance, reliability, and security.

As illustrated in Figure 1.2, SD-WAN is unfolding its great market potential as we speak. We will address each of the key characteristics of SD-WAN in specifics in the following chapters and sections of the book.

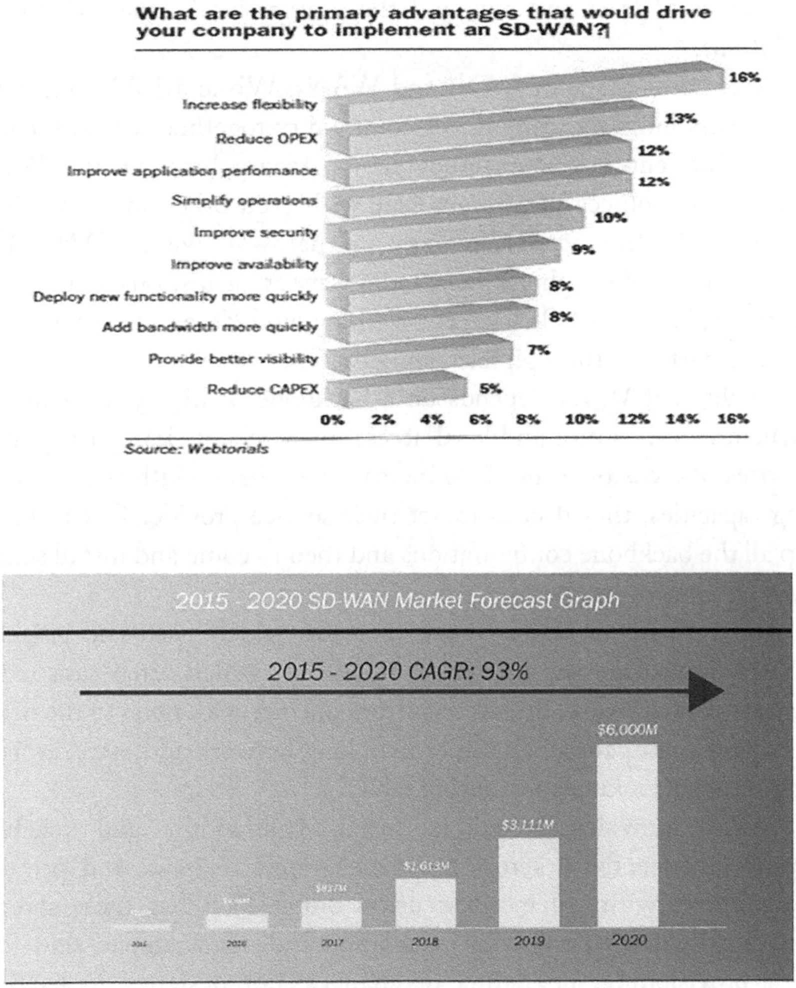

Figure 1.2 SD-WAN drivers (Source: Webtorial) and market forecast. (Source: IDC.)

Then and Now

> "Being Smart and Efficient" makes the trademark for SD-WAN, which provides agility and flexibility, while maintaining centralized, predefined business policies controlling how applications get routed.

Before learning how SD-WAN takes place, we need to understand how the legacy WAN operates in concept and the core technologies that power SD-WAN, which makes it easier for us to tell the difference of then and now and the progressive journey of WAN solutions.

Network is made of LANs and WANs. While a LAN connects a business building, campus, or community together, a WAN connects different LANs together across geographical areas, allowing business offices to communicate with each other and providing access to the Internet. Technology and hardware wise, WAN relies on circuit-switched phone lines, radio wave transmissions, optic fiber technologies, MPLS/IP packet switching, and Ethernet connections to transport data through telecom networks.

Traditional WAN depends on a backbone of highly mechanical structure and control and local access to the client sites via physical devices. If a customer needs to increase their bandwidth above existing capacities, they'll need to get their service provider first to tune up all the backbone configurations and then to come and install some new equipment on site.

For the past 15 and 20 years, the most widely used and reliable WAN technology for enterprises is MPLS, which often runs over private data network, directs data from one network node to the next based on short path labels rather than long network addresses, avoiding complex lookups in a routing table.

MPLS provides incredible speed, bandwidth, and reliable uptime, connectivity across broad geographical areas, and private connections with enhanced security. But MPLS has these shortfalls: costly and complex for installation and management; slow for new provisioning, upgrading or changes; not designed to handle Cloud and mobile data traffic well.

Thus, the challenges for the next-generation WAN are, functionality wise, how to maintain the strengths of the traditional WAN while overcoming its shortfalls. Services and application wise, as already described earlier, the next-gen WAN needs to address service requirements from Cloud computing, mobile data, and IoT.

SD-WAN Being the Smart New WAN

Now SD-WAN, often deployed as an overlay of the public Internet routes, comes on board to fulfill these gaps with lower prices, direct Cloud links, and reduced complexity, plus it also offers higher uptime, better application performance, security, and faster network operations. This strategically adds consumer grade broadband Internet into the corporate WAN play. Businesses can quickly create a smart "hybrid WAN" that comprises IP VPN, broadband Internet, and wireless services. The smart WAN will steer and shape traffic automatically and dynamically across the most appropriate WAN path based on network conditions, the security, and QoS requirements of the applications.

The innovative technologies behind SD-WAN change the long-haul transmission paradigm from a quasi-dumb packet-based network routing system to a smart application-based routing platform. It uses dynamic WAN selection to route those apps over the best-performing pathways, with an "active/active" configuration to provide load balancing and failover. Traffic between sites flows over dynamic, fully encrypted tunnels and can be segmented, providing for a high level of security.

"Being Smart and Efficient" makes the trademark for SD-WAN, which provides agility and flexibility, while maintaining centralized, predefined business policies controlling how applications get routed. The resulting visibility and control it provides allows the customer or service provider to identify applications running across the WAN and set policies on their prioritization and use.

SDN/NFV Shapes SD-WAN Paradigm

> While NFV enables the efficient and simplified structure, SDN triggers the intelligence to run the new network structure. SDN and NFV provide freedom to flexibly manage networks and simplify the infrastructure.

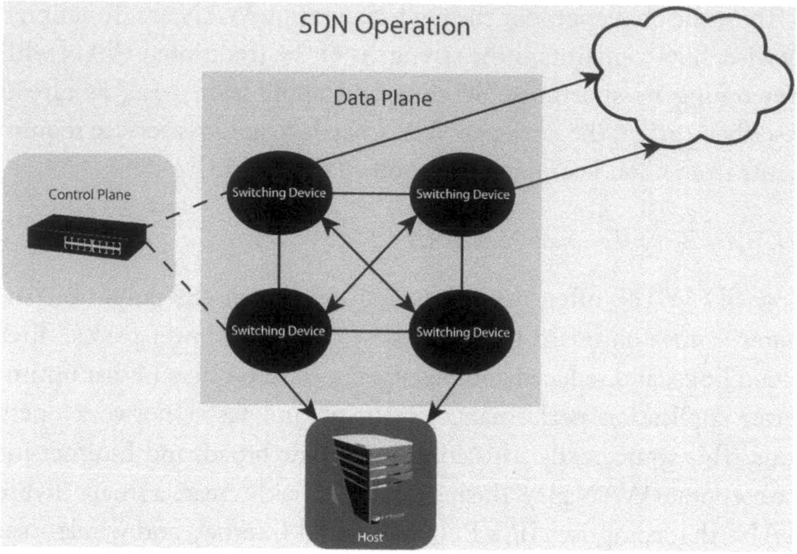

Figure 1.3 How SDN works.

What makes SD-WAN smart and efficient? The two core technologies that power SD-WAN are software-defined networking (SDN) and network functions virtualization (NFV). As illustrated in Figure 1.3, together they are creating a new paradigm and platform of WAN network operations.

To better understand SDN/NFV, we can start from the decoupling of control plane and data (forwarding) plane in the network. Control and forwarding planes are part of key network management elements. Traditionally they are bonded together into a physical hardware device like a switch or router. Then these hardware devices are installed and scattered across the network, so as to route IP packets from one point to another.

The control plane significantly defines the topology of a network. It can be called "the brains of the router" and is responsible for establishing links between routers and for exchanging protocol information. Data Plane (Forwarding Plane), on the other hand, follows the logic established by control plane and forwards traffic to the next hop along the path to the selected destination network.

SDN originally defines an approach to designing, building, and managing networks from the separated network's control plane. This approach enables the network control to become directly programmable and the underlying infrastructure to be abstracted for applications and network services.

NFV is different from SDN but it works closely with SDN and makes many virtual machines (VMs) of network functions in software mode possible, running over a shared and simplified hardware platform. Together SDN/NFV lifts network traffic routing, management, and provisioning to the next level. While NFV enables the efficient and simplified structure, SDN triggers the intelligence to run the new network structure. SDN and NFV provide freedom to flexibly manage WAN networks.

NFV abstracts the network functions, such as routing, switching, security management, DNS, caching, etc., from proprietary hardware appliances, so they can run in software to accelerate service innovation and provisioning, particularly within a service provider's environment.

Hence SDN, with the support of NFV, offers a centralized and programmable network that can dynamically provision so as to address the changing needs of businesses. It adds or modifies virtual network functions first in the central control plane and then the functions can be quickly distributed through to the data plane of local devices for implementation with high efficiency.

When using public Internet as the underlay, SDN architecture provides an improved and secure connectivity, overcoming many shortfalls of the public Internet itself, allowing IT and other Operations teams to holistically manage the WAN, identify, and address service issues. It also provides automation and orchestration capabilities for further ease of management.

What's the relationship between SDN/NFV and SD-WAN? From the networking standpoint, SDN/NFV are the engines or enablers for the next-gen infrastructure, and SD-WAN is the customer-facing service appliance.

Specifically, SD-WAN focuses on providing software-defined application routing to the WAN, and on connecting an organization's geographically distributed locations, i.e., headquarters, data centers, branch offices, and remote and mobile users, on a national or global basis. While on the other hand, SDN/NFV focus internally on network enhancement, within the enterprise LAN or within the Service Provider's core network.

A Use Case: SDN Brings Smart and Efficient Network Control

SeaHawks Communications Corp is a major US national telecom carrier. Starting from mid-2012, they've started to adopt SDN/NFV for their network management and cost control. So far, they've benefitted tremendously from this strategic move in terms of network control, security, and business growth.

From a service agility standpoint, SDN allows SeaHawks Communications to manage the network capacity on demand, and lower the risks associated with rolling out new services. They can easily trial and evolve services to determine what best meets the needs of customers. It's also easier for SeaHawks to provision new services to support a seasonal marketing campaign or ad-hoc research and development project upon customers' demand.

For network security, SDN lets Seahawks more easily deploy updates and isolate and contain problems. In case a Distributed Denial of Service (DDoS) attack happens, for example, its goal is to flood and block certain key service gateways in a network. In their quick response to security breach, SeaHawk's team can use its software-centric architecture to scale the network security in near real time or set up failover routing to avoid disruption to the network operations.

From business and commercial perspectives, SDN/NFV enables Seahawks to reduce the time to deploy new networking services to support changing business requirements, seize new market opportunities with fast response against competitions, improve return on investment (ROI) of new services, and lower the total cost of network ownership by eliminating the need for proprietary equipment and devices purchasing.

What Differences Does SD-WAN Make in Service?

> SD-WAN can be deemed more as a complement or hybrid solution to MPLS services depending on the enterprise client's specific needs and applications.

As already mentioned, the most popular incumbent WAN solution is MPLS, sometimes called private IP. There's a significant amount of business that is on MPLS-based backbones over T1 or fast Ethernet level access today, but that's also where enterprise clients need a significantly bigger bandwidth and speed, via public Internet backbone network over diverse access options with security and at less cost. That's where SD-WAN will shine.

MPLS debuted about 15 years ago to replace then-popular Frame-Relay and ATM for WAN solutions. While MPLS provides enterprises with a private national or global network that mitigates performance problems inherent in public Internet and IP SEC WAN solutions, it is still not a perfect answer to branch connectivity and is gradually getting out of date in the face of the emerging digital transformation.

Today, SD-WAN offers a head-on hit on the MPLS drawbacks. Depending on the sophistication of the provider, SD-WAN can be launched immediately (whereas MPLS typically takes months to be provisioning) and manage congestion, packet-loss, and security issues associated with the public Internet. With SD-WAN, enterprises gain access to Internet links with points of presence all over the country or globe that directly connect regional or international offices, bypassing the congested middle-mile in the typical MPLS bub-spoke topology.

A Quick Comparison

If we take a close look at Figure 1.4, we can find three distinctions between the MPLS and SD-WAN architecture. First, the SD-WAN architecture is simpler with less hardware devices. Second, SD-WAN has a central controller that makes the networking more intelligent. Third, SD-WAN works as an overlay, agnostically on top of all existing WAN infrastructures.

On the other hand, while SD-WAN is disruptive, it is not replacing the traditional WAN, especially MPLS in every scenario. It can be deemed more as a complement or hybrid solution to MPLS services depending on the enterprise client's specific needs and applications.

To sum up, SD-WAN can take advantage of both MPLS and public Internet, while overcoming their shortfalls by offering the following capabilities and features:

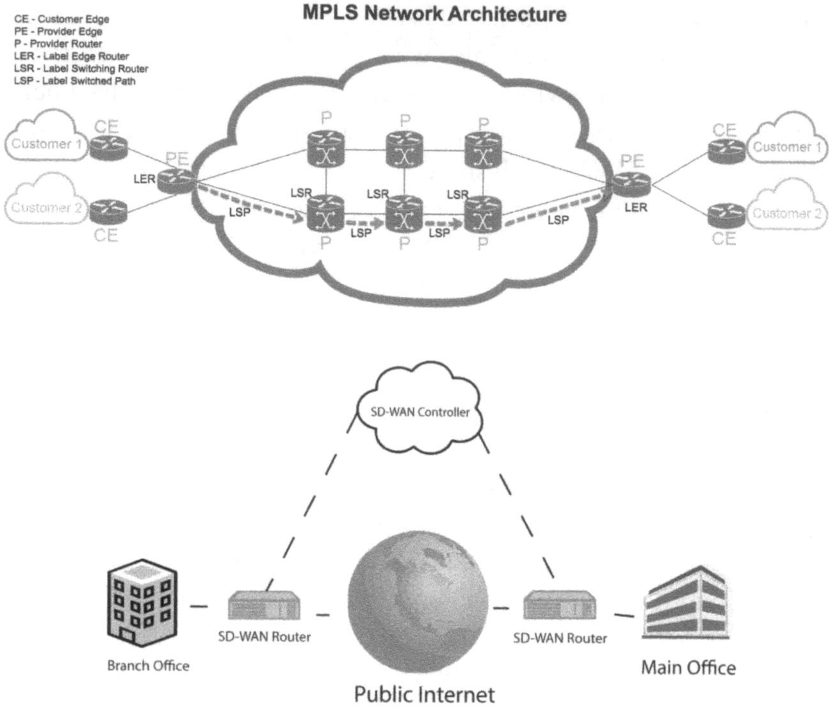

Figure 1.4 MPLS vs. SD-WAN.

Increased Bandwidth with Price Reduction There's no question that MPLS services are more expensive than public Internet service on top of which SD-WAN runs and operates. On average, MPLS services are significantly higher than Internet services in term of cost, probably close to 30% or more. A large part of the pricing depends on the port size on demand, the particular route in selection in term of cost, type of Class of Service (CoS) being implemented by the MPLS service, whether fiber already exists or not at the location, and other factors.

With MPLS, if a client needs 100M+ bandwidth, the monthly circuit costs will often become barely affordable, sometimes from the router and device costs and long lead time for installation, and sometimes from the circuit installation themselves.

SD-WAN, however, allows the client to utilize multiple, high-bandwidth, inexpensive Internet connections over business-class cable, fiber, 4G, etc. or make an Internet+MPLS hybrid. Aggregating multiple connections lead to fast connection speed at a low cost.

Enterprise Users Having More Control With MPLS, the enterprise must have the same MPLS service provider at all sites, making it an all-or-nothing relationship.

As a result, the bar for switching the MPLS provider is pretty high and the process quite painful. A client is easily stuck and locked up with an MPLS provider. With SD-WAN being network agnostic, an end user won't get stuck with a certain service provider anymore and can add and remove a connection option at any site, any time, with ease.

With MPLS, there is only one network connection and the CoS settings are static, without the ability to adjust on short notice. At a minimal extent, with SD-WAN, the end user will depend less on a service provider than it did before. Now many firms are reducing the size of their MPLS network subscription for their real-time applications, instead adding SD-WAN as the front connection using MPLS as a backup.

Performance That Counts This is where SD-WAN and MPLS have a head-on competition. As a managed service often over a secured and managed private network, MPLS ports bring lower latency and packet loss and better uptime than Internet connections. The routing policies of an MPLS service will be designed for maximum performance from standard, silver to gold levels. All performance characteristics of MPLS will be backed with SLAs.

Although nowadays SD-WAN performance over Internet backbone can often show packet loss rates comparable to that of MPLS network, public Internet performance is known as less predictable due to spikes in Internet loss and oversubscription in the access layer. But again SD-WAN now through centralized and intelligent routing control over redundant lines can better cope with such issues.

With regard to network latency, the rates will also vary and on average will be higher with an SD-WAN over public Internet than with MPLS services. The rule of thumb is metro and regional Internet backbone closer to major Internet Exchanges can nearly match the private network performance, while national and international routes may not, especially in some developing countries and areas.

SD-WAN may fall short due to some out of control issues, and Internet routing may show gaps between the service provider's business requirements and customer requirements. Least cost vs. optimal path may impact a service provider's network routing selections. Peering vs. transit can also make a difference when packets would be better served traversing another provider's backbone, while peering may have some performance restrictions. We will address this subject in more detail in Chapter 3.

Serving Small and Remote Sites Nearly every company has sites which are not a good fit for their MPLS network because they are either too small to justify the high cost of an MPLS circuit, or they are not serviceable by their MPLS provider's network. In these locations, companies with MPLS are typically forced to suffer through less-than-desirable performance as they run all traffic over an IPsec VPN.

To the contrary, SD-WAN enjoys more advantages in serving small and remote sites: It can throttle low-priority traffic over dual ISP connections and always send the traffic across the Internet circuit with the fastest route. SD-WAN's central orchestration will better condition the traffic at a higher transport quality.

Availability and Redundancy MPLS services come with SLAs governing time to deliver the service, downtime, time to repair, and more. MPLS uptime is typically much higher, on the order of 99.99% per year especially over fiber and redundant connections. SD-WAN can offer similar SLA too now over most metro and regional networks in the US. MPLS providers sometimes have a failover to a secondary Internet connection but it's typically not instantaneous as SD-WAN can offer.

In terms of network blackout and brownout, MPLS has little concerns due to its nature of private network. For public Internet, the complete failures of an Internet connection may not happen all the time, but intermittent slowdowns are common. Sometimes rerouting will be available but at significantly downgraded performance with increasing packet loss and latency while reducing throughput.

SD-WAN now can better handle such access layer outages and brownouts. By aggregating multiple ISP Internet and WAN connections at a single site, SD-WAN will manage to provide seamless circuit redundancy for the customer WAN, across multiple circuit types and service provider networks.

A Use Case of SD-WAN Replacing MPLS in Phases

General Trader Corp is a large enterprise handling industrial raw material with 500 global sites including central and branch offices employing over 5,200 people globally. In mid-2017, the firm adopted SD-WAN which is not only saving money on the MPLS service they used before, but the company is able to deploy new applications as well that it couldn't accomplish before due to the restraints of old technologies.

General Trader IT group has been struggling to keep up with their MPLS service because the executive team has the pressure down for them to spend less for doing more. But in managing their current MPLS service, just adding the capacity that they needed for existing and new sites already spent tons of money. The prompt for their adoption of SD-WAN actually was triggered by their upcoming renewal of its existing MPLS contract with an established service provider.

After running intensive analysis of its current and future networking demands and whether MPLS would be enough to support a technological evolution, they determined that the current network would be unable to scale to support a shift in corporate dependency on Cloud applications and services such as Office365, Salesforce.com, and file storage while providing the same level of experience to all branches and offices.

SD-WAM thus became a better and viable option on the radar for their business growth. After some insightful and intensive negotiation, the company picked a managed service provider who deploys SD-WAN as a phased replacement to the existing MPLS infrastructure. What they did is they still renewed the MPLS service but on a smaller scale of bandwidth for each site, and then added SD-WAN as hybrid solution. The managed SD-WAN saved significant money compared to if General Trader would totally renew the legacy MPLS service.

General Trader also immediately saw benefits in terms of better WAN performance and user experience. For example, the flexibility inherent in SD-WAN of direct Cloud service access, and multiple deployment models such as a hybrid of broadband and MPLS or 4G LTE, or fully broadband. This provides a sound migration approach for General Trader. For Day One, the company chose a hybrid architecture because of their investment in an existing MPLS infrastructure as well as broadband Internet backup. Next step, General Trader's goal is to eliminate their dependency on the established backbone and migrate to a full broadband dependent SD-WAN platform.

SD-WAN and Its Major Components

> SD-WAN is an intelligent WAN, overcoming many shortfalls of the dumb public Internet, hence making it feasible as an enterprise network backbone solution.

As stated in above sections, SD-WAN is much smarter than the dumb public Internet or the mechanical MPLS, and it allows for load sharing of traffic across multiple WAN connections in an efficient and dynamic fashion, with quick failover and security patching, and offloading Internet-destined traffic along the edge of the network to the Cloud.

Internet connectivity that SD-WAN runs over is far less expensive than IP VPNs and can be extended to anywhere public IP is available or portable, and SD-WANs are also far easier to use and manage than MPLS VPNs that require implementation of Border Gateway Protocol (BGP). For enterprises, SD-WAN overlay can be a boon.

The SD-WAN Solution Portfolio

According to the Metro Ethernet Forum (MEF), in general the SD-WAN managed service components include edge devices, central controller, service orchestrator, and user web portal, as illustrated in Figure 1.5.*

Edge devices are physical and vCPEs are deployed on the customer end. The edge devices initiate and terminate SD-WAN tunnel and perform application-based QoS and security policy enforcement. Sometimes for alternative VPN technologies, e.g., Carrier Ethernet or MPLS VPNs, an SD-WAN gateway may be needed for

* MEF: Understanding SD-WAN Managed Services issued in July 2017.

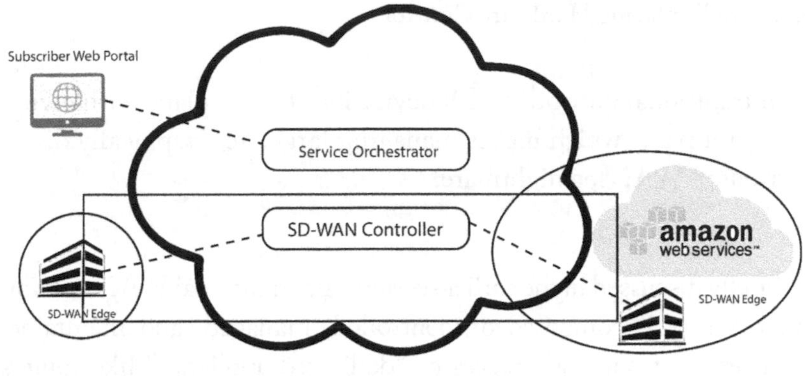

Figure 1.5 SD-WAN service components.

interconnections. But such a gateway may not be able to perform the typical SD-WAN functions like application-based forwarding.

The SD-WAN Central Controller sets up the SD-WAN overlay tunnel and provides physical or virtual device management for all SD-WAN Edges and Gateways associated with the controller. The central controller handles activities like configuration and activation, IP address management, and routing policies onto SD-WAN Edges and SD-WAN Gateways.

The SD-WAN Service Orchestrator provides the overall management of the SD-WAN service lifecycle including service fulfillment, performance, control, assurance, usage, analytics, security, and policy. SD-WAN central controller and service orchestrator take advantages of SDN/NFV and are the major differentiators with the traditional data network.

After the SD-WAN service is activated, the User Web Portal communicates with the Service Orchestrator and allows for SD-WAN service modifications such as setting up different QoS, security, or business policies as long as the user or administrator is authorized to modify the SD-WAN service.

In a nutshell, SD-WAN has greatly simplified the legacy WAN structure and command-line interfaces (CLI) that most folks are familiar with to date and made the networking process smart, agile, and responsive, hence making it a feasible enterprise network backbone solution. In the following sections, we will highlight three major and disruptive features from SD-WAN: Software replacing hardware control, virtual network fabric/overlay in architecture, and centralized orchestration and security.

Software Replacing Hardware Control

> In traditional networks, each device has its data plane with own control plane which makes managing large, geographically distributed WANs, a nightmare.

As briefly discussed in the earlier section, the traditional WAN network functionality is composed of, controlled, managed, and maintained via a series of hardware pieces or "dedicated appliance" like routers, switches, gateways, firewalls, accelerators, CPEs, and each device has a data plane with its own control plane—which makes managing large, geographically distributed WANs, a nightmare. The market, enterprise users, and service providers are increasingly confronted with the limitations of this hardware-centric approach for WAN communications.

Configuration in a hardware-centric network can be time-consuming and error-prone. Many steps are needed when an IT administrator needs to make a change, such as adding or removing a single device in a traditional network. Such work includes the manual configuration of a network device on an individual basis, using device-level management tools to update numerous configuration settings, such as ACLs (access control lists), BGPs, and QoS.

To make things worse, the average customers own a variety of equipment of different vendors or in a multi-vendor environment, which requires a high level of expertise in configuration and management.

Such a configuration approach makes it harder and more complex to deploy a consistent set of policies, especially over a large size of network. From the security standpoint, in case of a compromised device, this approach risks giving external exposure to the entire network and slowing network administrators from responding to security breaches. As a result, network security breaches and noncompliance may often occur, which interferes with meeting business networking needs.

The connectivity evolution such as IoT that is currently taking place further complicates things. In addition to tablets, PCs, and smartphones, other devices such as alarm systems, monitoring sensors, and security cameras are being linked to the Internet. The challenge is how to incorporate all these devices of different vendors within the network in a safe and structured manner.

To overcome these and other traditional networking limitations, SDN and NFV introduce a new perspective on network management, which is to run the next-gen network via software rather than hardware in a simplified network structure.

Their magic power comes from abstraction and decoupling—namely, the network management can be abstracted into a set of software-controlled capabilities that are completely independent of the hardware where those capabilities are implemented. As already mentioned in previous sections, the abstraction becomes possible due to NFV and SDN can decouple a control plane from a data plane and manage it from a software defined, automatic, and programmable ecosystem.

In SD-WAN, for instance, there is only one central control plane to rule all data planes—putting the power back in the control center's hands in orchestrating and handling configuration, policy consistency, device add/remove, and security, no matter where those devices are and how large the network is. This is how SD-WAN providers enhance the network operation, management, and expense reduction to the next level of automation.

A Use Case of Hardware to Software Transition-vCPE

The current CPE deployment model of service providers requires multiple specialized devices at customer premises that take complicated on-site configuration, long installation hours, and high capex. Also, any changes and upgrading efforts in adding/removing CPEs are pains to cope with.

For a service provider, launching and deploying new services to enterprise customers can prove a significant challenge. If the core network infrastructure is inflexible, the service provider will incur higher CapEx and OpEx costs to physically install and provision services on CPE in each customer location. Plus, when a customer wants to change a service or add capacity, the service provider needs to go on-site again to reconfigure, update, or swap out the device.

From a customer's perspective, any change requires them to schedule time and wait for the service to be turned on, causing delays and revenue loss for their business. That can lead to lost revenues and lower customer satisfaction as well.

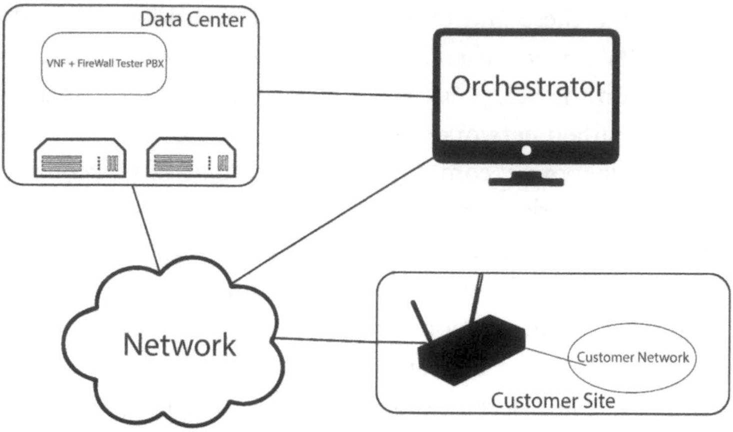

Figure 1.6 Cloud-based vCPE.

As illustrated in Figure 1.6, now vCPE can replace multiple hardware appliances with a generic "thin box" and plug-and-play level CPE or called Zero Touch Provisioning (ZTP), taking advantage of NFV infrastructures for services deployed in the Cloud and in the network, having work such as configuration, upgrading, and changes done remotely via SDN from a central control point, reducing both capex/opex.

vCPE therefore enables a Cloud and software defined model, which can share a common pool of resources and dynamically allocate physical compute and network resources to virtual network functions. For customers, vCPE will enable them to provision services on-demand and provide the required flexibility to rapidly scale up/down services and a consistent/superior QoS. Service providers on the other hand can deploy individual virtual instances of network functions (a firewall as an example) over vCPEs and offer them as on-premises services to the customer's location.

Integrated Master, Inc.'s, Experiences with vCPEs

Integrated Master, Inc., as a managed service solutions provider, recently has started to roll out their SD-WAN solution with vCPEs to their client's networks. Their SD-WAN offer is deployed including these features like load balancing as a service, firewall as a service, and DNS as a service.

Now via a self-service web portal that Integrated Master sets up, their enterprise customers can spin up or spin down instances of network functions or order new services that can be dynamically provisioned in a single location or multiple global locations in a short interval. Self-service allows the customers to move from the complexities, costs, and long delivery cycles associated with deploying physical devices to a Cloud-centric, automated, and agile model of on-demand service delivery.

Consequently, Integrated Master has achieved 45% TCO (total cost of ownership) saving, reduction in deployment of new CPEs, higher revenues from service monetization, and a higher ROI. vCPE helps to quickly introduce and deploy new network services, achieve end-to-end service automation and orchestration, and improve customer satisfaction and retention. As more virtual functions can be added and hosted, the firm has started to call their end devices as universal CPEs (uCPEs).

Virtual Fabric/Overlay in Network Architecture

> SD-WAN overlay promises major improvements in connectivity costs and WAN management without requiring massive changes to the existing network.

The SD-WAN overlay as illustrated in Figure 1.7, a layer higher than Layer 3, can be called IP Layer 3.5. It is a deployment method for SDN and NFV that runs a logically separate network or network component on top of existing infrastructure. This is also called infrastructure agnostic. Overlaying an SD-WAN on existing connectivity is most common and popular now, because it promises major improvements in connectivity costs and WAN management without requiring massive changes to the existing network environment.

Specifically, SD-WAN overlay technology uses OpenFlow-enabled hypervisor virtual switches at the server access layer of a network to create a virtual network on top of an existing physical network. Each user then gets a generic thin box or software element at each site, and that box terminates "tunnels" or overlay connections over which the user's VPN traffic is carried.

The cons for overlay networking, however, include hiding a lot of lower-layer stuff from view. The legacy underlay still has to be

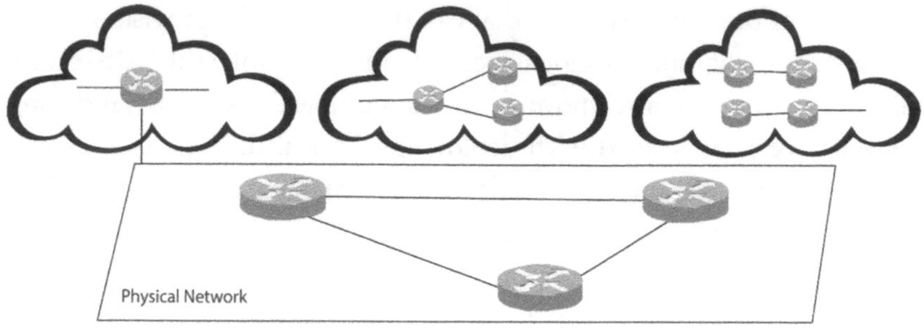

Figure 1.7 Network overlay fabric.

maintained, managed, and monitored to some extent though. The branch stack may get one box deeper, and the data-center network also becomes more complex.

To overcome the cons above, one thing worth mentioning is the SDN/NFV-driven trend of network disaggregation for many service providers, meaning the overlay doesn't need to be always separate with the underlay structure. Rather SDN/NFV makes it possible to gradually replace, integrate, and simplify some underlay work functions and transcending the whole infrastructure to next level and get rid of the boxes. In the long run, it will save hassles to maintain, manage, and monitor the legacy network.

As a value add, some SD-WAN systems (such as via the new uCPEs) can replace other device boxes as well, such as firewalls and optimizers. Overall the transition on network disaggregation is more complex. In case anything goes wrong, it is harder to back out of a replacement than an overlay and thus may cause a whole network blackout. A sound approach is for service providers to get the high-level benefits of SD-WAN right away and handle disaggregation and replacement one at a time.

A Use Case: SD-WAN Overlay Provides Flexibility and Saving

The SD-WAN overlay using multiple links from multiple providers gives the enterprise client a higher level of redundancy and application-QoS than what a traditional WAN architecture can offer. For many enterprises, they may already have some public Internet access circuits handy for backup purpose which often sit their idle in routine mode. Now they can start to use these links for SD-WAN in a dynamic active-active mode.

Additionally, SD-WAN is self-healing by nature of SDN/NFV, and as such, can typically survive degraded links, and even full outages with very little to no impact on application performance.

The SD-WAN overlay implementation doesn't require any internal "nodes", and in effect the sites are fully meshed. The overlay tunnels through the physical network make it possible to build a software-defined network on top of existing infrastructure.

As a good example, if an enterprise needs 1Gig throughput with protection on their WAN, they no longer need a 1G primary link and 1G failover link. With an SD-WAN, they can pay for a 500 mbps primary link and 500 mbps failover link either vial Internet hybrid, or dual Internet, and yet, their WAN will perform at 1G speeds, due to the aggregation and load balancing of all available bandwidth into a single pool. This is where the cost saving starts to happen from SD-WAN.

Centralized Control, Orchestration, and Provisioning

> The most crucial element of SDN orchestration is the ability to monitor the complex network, optimize and automate connectivity.

After hardware and software separation and the establishment of overlay network mostly from NFV, then SDN starts to do its own magic: centralized control and orchestration, which is the ability to monitor the complex network, optimize and automate connectivity. Now via open source program such as OpenDaylight, SDN orchestration can coordinate with an SDN controller, which is programmed to make automate decisions about the network, in the case of traffic congestion, faulty devices, or security problems.

Centralized orchestration or called Lifecycle Service Orchestration (LSO), as illustrated in Figure 1.8, is considered one of the most promising growth areas of SDN networks and software systems. Its platforms are made of many types of proprietary or open source software, running on a number of network protocols including OpenFlow and IP-based networking, using common APIs (application program interface) that can tie into standard networking technologies.

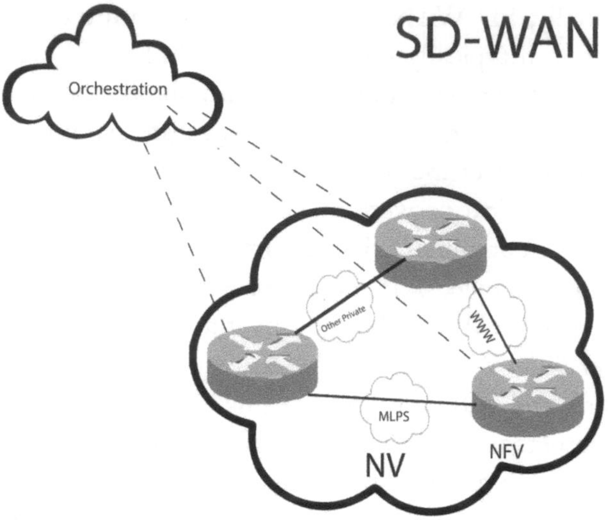

Figure 1.8 Centralized services orchestration.

Nowadays global service providers are adopting LSO software that integrates orchestration, fulfillment, control, performance, assurance, usage, analytics, security, and policy of enterprise networking services based on open and interoperable standards. Latest market research projects the total opportunity for LSO technologies in enterprise service offerings will approach $2.75 billion by 2019.*

SDN orchestration systems is paving the way for network automation and will provide the important "glue" between a wide range of technologies that automate Cloud-based network and communications services. SDN powered network coordination and automation would bridges the gap between telecom systems, data-center resources, OSS systems, and the customers looking to purchase Cloud-based technology and network services.

Using service order fulfillment as an example, after the order generation either manually or online, SDN orchestration technology would automatically get into provisioning the service. Based on the service order requirement, the automation may handle provisioning activities including virtual network layers setup, server-based virtualization, best routing selection, vCPE configuration, or security services such as encrypted tunnel.

* Rayno Report released in March 2015.

Enhanced Security from SD-WAN as a Use Case

A typical use case for centralized connectivity control and orchestration is to give customers or service providers the power to enforce security policies from a single central NOC (network operation center) or web portal. This may include setting up policies and security restrictions and managing network traffic and launching new branches accordingly. Such capabilities will effectively address the concerns customers may have over security when SD-WAN runs over the public Internet.

As a standard feature, most SD-WAN solutions enable encryption tunnels across virtual private network (VPN) security based on the industry standard IPsec with AES 128 or 256 encryption. Every IP packet that leaves the network is encrypted and encapsulated into a new IP packet with a new IP header, making it virtually impossible to intercept data, which results in a resilient, secure VPN backbone between all the service sites. With the right SD-WAN implementation, and the service provider knowing well how to respond quickly in case of a security breach, the odds of a breach are getting low.

In addition, SD-WAN has many advanced security features such as next-gen fire walls and antivirus via 3rd party vendor service chaining, particularly for multi-site businesses. Users can log into a secure dashboard in the service web portal to monitor and administer the network remotely, ensuring there are no "weak links" to jeopardize company data. Security protocols are automatically applied to new equipment, ensuring the network stays secure as it grows.

SD-WAN's Role in Digital Transformation

> On the ICT platform, there is an ongoing convergence of five key technologies that are poised to transform the world, including SD-WAN and 5G cellular.

Digital transformation, as demonstrated in Figure 1.9, is the profound transformation of business and organizational activities, processes, competencies, and models to fully leverage the changes and opportunities of a mix of digital technologies. The transformation is already

Figure 1.9 The digital transformation.

underway and will accelerate impact across society in a strategic and dramatic way, triggering many shifts in mind and action.

For enterprises, digital transformation enables technology to radically change the performance or service reach of a business. Boundaries between office and work and customer and supplier are also getting murky, which brings about a fundamental rethinking about the role of technology and its relations with humans in organizations.

The Information and Communications Technology (ICT) ecosystem is the major driver and glue of digital transformation. On the ICT platform, there is an ongoing convergence of five key technologies that are poised to transform the world. These technologies are SDN/NFV powered network including SD-WAN and 5G cellular, Cloud-edge computing, AI, Big Data Analytics, and the IoT.

Each of these technologies will have a huge impact in their own right, both on ICT as well as on all major industry verticals that depend on ICT services. However, the combination of these technologies will create more opportunities to significantly impact and enhance user experiences for communications, applications, digital content, and commerce.

For instance, on October 30, 2017, a piece of news came up: **AT&T Introduces AI platform, Makes It Open Source,*** which announced AT&T just launched a Platform as a Service (PaaS) via Cloud for enabling IT developers to easily build, share, and deploy AI (e.g., machine learning) applications.

* Light Reading: AT&T Launches Open Source AI Platform, October 30, 2017.

Furthermore, this is where AI and SD-WAN click together: AT&T is leveraging **Indigo**, its next-gen platform for delivering a seamless network experience to support the PaaS AI solution. **Indigo** is a version of SD-WAN—software-defined and data-powered networking that also includes faster Internet speeds.

Indeed, if there is one thing that's clear in digital transformation, it's that all the technologies above are working together to push one another forward, creating a swell of change that simply cannot be resisted.

With regard to the particular role of SD-WAN in this digital transformation, NFV and SDN are the fuel, software and Cloud define the route, and customer experiences interact with the ongoing results. In the following sections, we will examine how SD-WAN would work together with unified communications (UCs), Cloud-edge computing and IoT, AI, and Big Data Analytics.

Working with UCaaS

> Cloud-delivered SD-WAN can assure the UC quality and deliver WAN visibility, reliability, and security that a private link provides.

UC as illustrated in Figure 1.10 is a popular enterprise communication solution that unifies separate modes of communication into a single, combined user experience. Email, text, and voice messaging work seamlessly with Web collaboration and live voice, audio, and video conferencing, in one interface, with "presence" notification to indicate the user's availability to participate.

Special UC features like a finger swipe lets the user move between tablet, smartphone, or desktop phones, while One Number Service lets calls follow the user to whatever device selected—whether office, home, or outing lodge—completely transparent to the caller. Also, UC nowadays can be integrated or embedded into business process software like ERP and Salesforce.com.

Businesses have deployed UC solutions on-premises for years. With the advent of Cloud computing, enterprises are thinking favorably to host their UC applications into the Cloud. That was when UCaaS was introduced, however, with some shortfall in its networking segment.

Figure 1.10 Unified Communications as a Service (UCaaS).

When UCaaS was initiated, the service providers required customers to purchase a dedicated WAN connection such as a private line or MPLS to access the service, which introduced additional cost and complexity to the end customers. Although this on-net deployment allows the UCaaS providers to control WAN quality and assure the UC experience, alternatively more end customers are asking their UCaaS providers to support public Internet. However, the lack of QoS on broadband or Internet link can significantly impact UC performance quality and end user experience.

SD-WAN Comes to Rescue

SD-WAN plays a perfect role in bridging the gaps in UCaaS application network connectivity. The benefits of bundling SD-WAN with UCaaS are particularly significant for SMBs (small and medium sized business) who are falling behind in technology upgrade: an SD-WAN implementation reduces the complexity and downtime of UCaaS access for SMBs, and optimizes the costs associated with their outdated traditional WANs.

SD-WAN's smartness fits well to manage and optimize the traffic for each application offered by UCaaS, namely voice, email, and video would be treated and routed differently, with cost-conscious decisions about how to utilize various grades of bandwidth.

For SMBs, SD-WAN not only addresses the poor performance of the network but can also give much-needed clarity and direction to the company's Cloud strategy. Cloud-based UcaaS can be boosted by SD-WAN for branch offices as well, with improved QoS, stronger security, smooth interoperability, and increased visibility into traffic. Fundamentally, SD-WAN is upgrading SMBs and branch sites to the Cloud era.

Working with Cloud-Edge Computing and IoT

> Big data IoT must be powered by a dynamic and low-latency distributed network with smart edge computing and data center capabilities.

IoT, as illustrated in Figure 1.11, is a concept created in contrast to the notion that Internet connects people. By connecting devices, IoT generates data that help to create more friendly products, smarter insights, and better business results. It's stunning that as far back as 2008, the number of devices connected to the Internet already exceeded the number of people on Earth.

Fundamentally, an IoT solution is made of four major components: (1) the Thing—the device like a sensor or actuator; (2) the Local Network—this can include front mobile access, and a gateway translating proprietary communication protocols to IP, filtering and processing data, handling security, etc.; (3) the network backbone that hauls the IoT traffic via Internet, MPLS, or Ethernet; (4) the Cloud-based back-end Services including operation control centers, data processing systems, or interactive devices. IoT service therefore is more an ecosystem from device vendors, software vendors, IT service providers, telecom, and Cloud service providers, rather than a standalone solution.

At this stage, based on the report of Analysys Mason issued in June 2017,* the struggle the telcos are facing is while the revenue from complete IoT solutions (total spend including devices, applications,

* Analysys Mason: IoT VALUE CHAIN REVENUE: WORLDWIDE TRENDS AND FORECASTS 2016–2025, issued in Febuary 2017.

Figure 1.11 Internet of Things.

and connectivity, on IoT devices with an SIM) will exceed $200 billion in 2025 at CAGR of 18% worldwide, IoT connectivity revenue will only reach $28 billion by 2025 for the telcos, representing just 14% of the IoT total revenue pie. Hardware and software vendors are poised to grab the majority of IoT revenues away.

This is because most of IoT traffic today is in lower bandwidth and speed over wide areas, and the Industrial IoT often requires reliable and secured transport over the private but more expensive MPLS networks. To date, this IoT model of relatively small stream of traffic over the private IP network still plagues many telecom service providers from the cost and profit management perspective.

For the telcos to effectively capture the fast growing IoT business opportunities, they need to switch from a pure connectivity provider to an IoT platform aggregator, taking on and fulfilling these two strategic initiatives: enable and tailor the Big Data IoT vertical platforms via intelligent edge networking; reduce the cost and optimize their backbone network performance through SDN/NFV.

SD-WAN Pivotal to Telcos' Strategic IoT Transition

Different from the Lower Data IoT's "messenger role" that mostly just monitors and reports a device's status, Big Data IoT often plays a "platform role" in monitoring performance, processing data, responding to issues, and interacting with the front devices instantly.

The big data IoT vertical applications include industrial machinery (e.g., remote oil drilling), transportation equipment (cars, trains, and planes), health care equipment, precision agriculture/farming solutions, smart buildings, smart cities, smart utility grids, and future AI solutions.

Big data IoT therefore must be powered by a dynamic and low-latency distributed network with smart edge computing and data center capabilities, customizing to manage the IoT traffic pattern of vertical industries, respectively. This would allow data produced by IoT devices to be processed quickly and locally—closer to where it is created instead of routing across a long haul to the central data centers or Clouds.

The innovative architecture of SD-WAN can accommodate the scalability and flexibility required of Big Data IoT workloads, via implementing vCPEs on the edge. Operating as an agnostic network overlay directly linking to the Cloud, and abstracting network architectures over the wide area and distance.

vCPE virtualizes the functions of the local IoT gateway and leverages the edge Cloud computing capabilities in better managing the IoT traffic, facilitating effective data processing, simplifying the service provisioning, and providing tighter security.

Furthermore, SD-WAN's central orchestration and control capabilities are critical to IoT's successful deployment and operation. For example, while edge computing is getting popular, central Clouds will continue to serve as the core layer of the IoT service and can effectively support and backup the services to the edge.

All this requires the telcos to orchestrate, glue together, and manage the IoT solution bundle from a central point, integrating network services across the various device, mobile access, gateway, and Cloud-tier architectures. SD-WAN can serve as the glue for IoT services.

Working with AI and Big Data Analytics

> The combination of SDN and machine learning/AI is becoming a powerful tool for making WAN network smarter, securer, and more reliable.

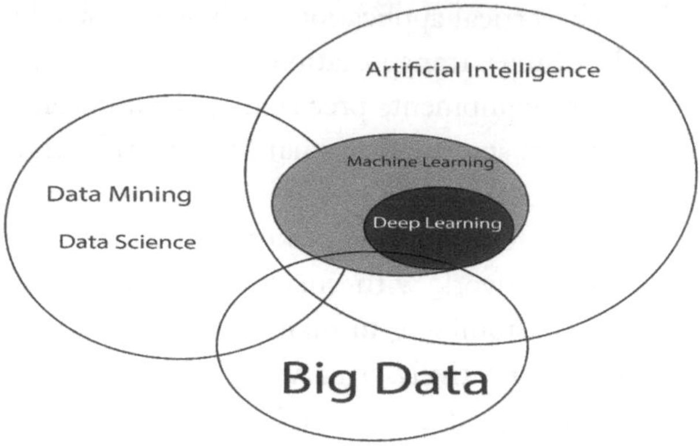

Figure 1.12 AI, machine learning & big data.

AI represents machine-based intelligence, as illustrated in Figure 1.12, typically manifest in "cognitive" functions that the human mind works along. The machine becoming cognitive is the key. Today many service providers have started using Machine Learning, one of the AI technologies which is made of self-learning systems that use data mining, pattern recognition, and natural language processing to mimic the way the human brain works.

Here are the fundamental three steps on how to apply AI and machine learning to business operation improvement: Step 1: Use data analytics to process vast amounts of machine-generated and often unstructured data. Step 2: Apply big data technologies and predictive analytics to stream lining, pattern recognition, and language interactions for information results. Step 3: Trigger and automate decision-making and improve ongoing efficiency and effectiveness of business operation.

The trend is the management of unstructured data (e.g., Big Data), the leveraging of analytics tools to derive value, and the integration between Cloud, IoT, and enterprise operational technology are becoming key focus areas for large companies across virtually every industry vertical.

From the network service and connectivity perspective, where SD-WAN falls under, AI is anticipated to have an ever increasing and integrated role for both traditional telecommunications as well as many communication enabled applications and digital commerce. The combination of SDN/NFV and machine learning/AI is becoming a powerful tool for making networks smarter, securer, and more reliable.

Al and big data analytics function as the brain for SDN, and Advanced Analytics delivers peak performance for SD-WAN, which can rapidly analyze massive volumes of information to detect patterns, trigger warnings, and find anomalies that can help network operators predict a range of network issues before they impact customers.

Telcos are Arming SD-WAN with AI

AI and machine learning in networking have become more useful as SD-WAN comes into play. For example, several telcos in Europe and North America are combining their human intelligence and seasoned networking experience, with machine learning and AI. This unprecedented synergy really starts to benefit the telcos in terms of network intelligence, CoS, security, trouble shooting, etc.

AI network management boosts telcos' tasks such as WAN path optimization, fault prediction, collection and analysis of centralized data, and distribution of network intelligence to the edge as well. Putting the intelligence at the edge allows the telcos to be able to detect and address issues or anomalies fast enough. Shorter mean time to repair could make a big difference in tackling a potential network malfunction or outage.

SD-WAN powered by AI network management will support new classes of highly demanding applications such as IoT. Thanks to its capabilities of application awareness, SD-WAN can create dedicated QoS lanes for the most mission-critical traffic, avoiding congestion by shifting traffic dynamically across multiple links including the public Internet.

With regard to SD-WAN security, being able to analyze data in motion, starting at the edge, is what makes rapid response possible and also enables a much higher degree of security. AI enables things like string analytics, advanced algorithms, machine learning—all of those things come into play. When AI finds a certain alignment of data matches a suspected threat profile, it will quickly trigger an alarm to the network, as well as the mechanism to quarantine or block traffic for security mitigation purposes.

For network troubleshooting and maintenance, AI can be used to monitor the behavior of the VMs and applications running in SDN and SD-WAN, so that when any issues or degradations are noticed, the decision can be quickly made on how to handle those issues. The current traffic patterns can then be compared to that baseline anytime in any format, in detecting anomalies that might trigger a troubling shooting response.

2
Adoption of SD-WAN Solutions

A Conversation with the CIO of a Mid-Size Enterprise

> I wish we could have gotten on board even earlier with SD-WAN.

I am curious about how the end users feel about SD-WAN as an innovative networking approach to delivering value to today's enterprises that are more digitized in applications and connectivity. Below is a dialogue I had with a CIO of a mid-size engineering equipment distribution firm that has adopted SD-WAN for network service.

Author (A): I know your firm is one of the early birds taking on SD-WAN solutions.

CTO (C): That is correct.

A: How do you feel about the service so far?

C: Super. I wish we could have got on board even earlier with SD-WAN.

A: What were the main drivers for you to adopt SD-WAN?

C: Two things for my firm in particular: cost saving and Cloud direct connections. As an engineering equipment distribution firm serving the North America market, we are HQed in Philadelphia and have about 30 office sites in the US and North America, including five in Canada and three in Mexico, plus couple of on site and data center IT operations. In the past, we paid about $70,000 monthly for MPLS services connecting all the sites. Now with SD-WAN, I can reduce our total network service cost to about $37,500 each month.

A: That's a big saving achieved. So you replaced MPLS with SD-WAN?

C: Not totally. Rather we still keep the MPLS links at regional level usually in Tier-1 or -2 cities but lower the bandwidth subscription significantly, like from 10 mbps to 5 mbps; meanwhile, still keep the 10G Ethernet links from the HQ to data centers.

A: That sounds quite a smart thing to do. Can we call it a hybrid solution?

C: Guess we can. Hybrid WAN used to mean a client uses two different service providers for recovery and redundancy purpose. Now with SD-WAN, it deepens this hybrid architecture with less cost though.

A: What happened to the connections for those Tier-3 city branch offices?

C: We've replaced MPLS with SD-WAN in many branch scenarios, although we would still subscribe to two Internet services from two different ISPs so as to keep the redundancy and failover capabilities there. Cost wise, two public Internet services are still lower than an MPLS connection.

A: So basically, you are paying less for doing more.

C: That's our goal. The other big driver for us to adopt SD-WAN is directly linking to the Cloud. Because most of my firm's software applications and data storage now are directly from the Cloud but MPLS and its hub-spoke structure is not designed to handle direct Cloud links well. In contrast, SD-WAN can do a wonderful job in this regard with 150 mbps or higher speed.

A: Any security concerns like PCI (Purchasing Card Industry) compliancy to your corporate network when linking employees directly to the Cloud without going through a central fire wall or security gateway anymore?

C: That was our concern before. But it turns out SD-WAN can offer and handle multiple secure access and entry points to our network and secure the traffic very well. It's just a matter of programming and implementing our security policies from the SD-WAN orchestration center. Then the SD-WAN security becomes part of our overall network security management.

A: I've heard SD-WAN's direct Cloud connection also help enterprises to simplify the branch IT operations and now can move many onsite services and devices to the Cloud.

C: That's true. I used to keep a minimum five person IT team on each branch office site to look after different servers and devices there. Now I can just use two IT persons each site while most of the operations can be controlled, managed, monitored, and maintained from our HQ's IT center into the Cloud.

A: What other SD-WAN features are attractive to your firm?

C: I would say fast new site provisioning or existing site change or upgrading. MPLS would take months to get such changes done while SD-WAN only takes days or hours. That's' a significant value-add to us.

A: I assume virtual CPE or so called white label capability over any 3rd party x86 hardware/devices are part of this fast provisioning process?

C: Yes. SDN and NFV makes vCPE and their software layer central control possible.

A: Last question, do you deploy SD-WAN by your own staff or you use a managed SD-WAN solution from a service provider?

C: We use a service provide to manage our SD-WAN solution so that my limited in-house IT staff can direct their attention more to our daily IT operation and services helping both internal employees and external partner or customers.

A: Sounds good. Thanks for this conversation. I wish we had more time to cover your SD-WAN adoption experiences which are helpful to other firms now checking into and considering SD-WAN services.

Why Adopt SD-WAN?

> Using public Internet as a WAN backbone was explored before but with little performance success and customer confidence. Now SD-WAN is making it possible and Internet also owns advantages of direct Cloud connections.

From a user perspective, an enterprise might have any or all of these following reasons for considering SD-WAN, which provides significant benefits compared to a traditional WAN and can result in capex

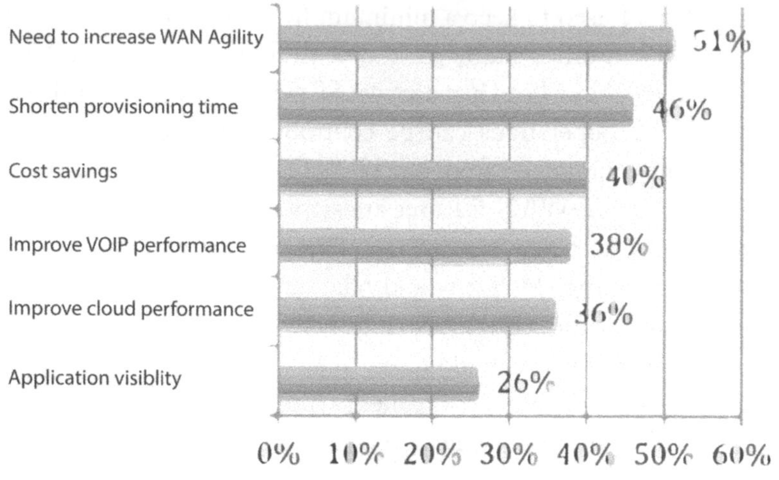

Figure 2.1 SD-WAN value propositions for enterprises.

and opex reduction. Every enterprise and its network is different but nearly every type can benefit from SD-WAN. For an enterprise that has a bigger WAN footprint, the more savings it may reap from SD-WAN. For SMBs, now SD-WAN enables them to effectively run most of their applications and daily operations from the Cloud.

In general, as illustrated in Figure 2.1, the SD-WAN attractions to the enterprises include cost saving and return on investment (ROI), public Internet utilization, Cloud connection, transport agnostic, branch office operation augmentation, management visibility, provisioning agility, and enhanced security.

Public Internet Utilization and Cloud Connectivity

Public Internet has the advantages of being cost effective, bandwidth scalable, and ubiquitously available; meanwhile, SD-WAN is capable of overcoming the security, reliability, and performance challenges to using the public Internet for business applications.

Transport Agnostic and Cost Saving

As already stated in the early sections, one of the chief characteristics of SD-WAN is its ability to manage multiple types of connections. Being able to mix different types of circuits—MPLS, broadband, cable, or even 4G LTE—and being able to support load balancing between multiple circuits at a branch, is helpful for augmenting enterprise bandwidth at the branch sites. In comparison, traditional WAN most of the time keeps an active circuit, while wasting money on a backup circuit which is often just idle, unless the primary circuit fails.

Application and Management Visibility

An enterprise might be looking to gain application visibility. SD-WAN technology has the ability to recognize all applications and configure them according to business requirements. The technology also makes it possible to see how applications are performing and what the user experience is and give priority to critical applications with increased agility.

Agility in Provisioning

SD-WAN is outstanding for the automation capabilities, which allows the users to handle provisioning like adding or removing devices on the network more quickly and cost-effectively. The user can make a configuration change on thousands of branches in a very short time compared to the traditional long lead time in deploying the configuration at individual branches.

Security

A big benefit of SD-WAN is the ability to increase segmentation, where each segment can have a different topology, thus increasing security in the network. All of the enterprise critical or sensitive applications or devices can be in a separate segment. So, for example, if a firm's branches handle credit card transactions that must comply with PCI or healthcare private data that must comply with HIPAA, the network administrator can isolate this sensitive traffic by keeping it in a separate segment for better security treatment.

SD-WAN Business Case and ROI

> Companies should be able to easily calculate the payback period that is associated with SD-WAN implementations at a high level.

As mentioned in Chapter 1, MPLS or IP VPN is a mature network product for most service providers as by far the most widely available international enterprise network service. But the market and industry are witnessing an increasing pace of IP VPN price erosion which reflects growing competition. In order to gain the competitive edge, service providers are taking such measures as expanding footprints for their economy of scale, reducing underlying transport costs with SDN/NFV, adding AI/machines learning and vCPE technologies, and launching new cost-effective alternatives like SD-WAN.

A decision on SD-WAN adoption and implementation is a big step for enterprises, and often determining the ROI needs to happen first in the planning process, so that the management can obtain some good idea on the benefits and savings from SD-WAN in terms of performance, security, and money amount before making a final decision.

When building a business case for any kind of investment in IT, the two types of savings an enterprise can realize are tangible savings and non-tangible savings. Tangible savings refer to a verifiable reduction in spending, such as the reduction that results from canceling an MPLS circuit used for the current WAN. Non-tangible savings refer to benefits like improved productivity or better compliance. Since non-tangible savings are harder to measure and more difficult to use as justification for an investment in IT, most business cases will focus on tangible savings, as indicated by Figure 2.2 as an example.

Costs for SD-WAN

Example: Three-Year Costs for 250-Branch WAN		
Item	Traditional	SD-WAN
Router Capex	$1,000,000	$250,000
Router Maint/Support	$180,000	$150,000
Staffing Opex	$105,000	$52,500
Total	$1,285,000	$452,500

Figure 2.2 A sample of cost savings on SD-WAN.

For an enterprise, there are many factors that go into calculating the total cost of an SD-WAN solution. Unfortunately, there isn't a standard price list of SD-WAN yet because no company's network/IT architecture is the same. Typically, however, organizations need to delve into a few of the following key factors for consideration before nailing down the budget for SD-WAN adoption.

Network Size: How large is the current network, i.e., # of sites? What is the data center to location ratio? Any plan to add or reduce sites?

Branches: How dispersed is the workforce such as remote and mobile workers? How important is reliable contact between the branches? Does each branch have many existing servers and CPEs to manage?

Network Infrastructure: Are Cloud applications important and mainstream? In case of any Cloud migration, will that happen in the near future? How much traffic is directed to MPLS and Internet, respectively? Is the current WAN static or optimized?

Data: Is the firm's data sensitive and highly regulated? What kind of employee/customer data travels the firm's system? What's the average bandwidth and speed demand for the firm's data transport? How is network traffic flow managed currently?

An SD-WAN Case of ROI Assessment

Adachea Inc.—a multinational accounting firm—has 250 branch offices and averages two T1 links to an MPLS service from each office, at a monthly average cost of $550 per T1. The firm spends $4,000 on router purchasing and installation for each site as capex, with $380 annually on router maintenance and onsite staffing support for each site.

To measure the benefits of SD-WAN adoption and business case, Adachea applies payback period, which defines the amount of time before the resultant savings equal or exceed the cost of deploying a new technology or service.

Assume that by implementing SD-WAN, Adachea can, on average, reduce one T1 link at each branch office and replace it with a high-speed broadband Internet link, with

- an average monthly cost of $50.
- a monthly savings of $500 per branch office.

- a total monthly savings of $125,000 from all the branch MPLS replacements.
- $750,000 capex saving from regular CPE replacement with vCPEs.
- $110 saving annually on router maintenance and onsite staffing support for each site.

To demonstrate how to calculate the payback period, here are the three major steps:

Step One—Assume the SD-WAN that Adachea will implement costs $720,000;

Step Two—Implementing SD-WAN will result in monthly savings of $120,000, and

Step Three—Adachea gains a payback period of six (6) months—using $720,000 divided by $120,000 in savings per month.

A high-level summary of this Business Case of Adachea, Inc. adoption of SD-WAN can be shown as the following:

- Projected ROI in only 6 months.
- Monthly connection costs to be reduced by over $125,000.
- Dependence on costly MPLS connection to be reduced.
- Site deployment time to be reduced by nearly 100%.
- If the firm plans for additional five MPLS sites, then using SD-WAN as an alternative can save extra $2,500 monthly.

Anyhow, companies should be able to easily calculate the payback period that is associated with SD-WAN implementations at a high level. At a minimum, the analysis provides the company with greater insight into whether adopting SD-WAN will result in tangible savings and hopefully would help trigger a decision making of SD-WAN transition from the senior executives.

Synchronizing with Cloud Applications

> The Cloud app growth has also caused businesses to think differently when deploying long distance networks, or WANs, as traditional technologies like MPLS were not built for the Cloud.

Much as predicted and expected, Cloud application adoption has increased exponentially these recent years—voice, data, video, and collaboration tools are increasingly moving to the Cloud for companies of all sizes. The forecast shows $78.43 billion in Software as a Service (SaaS) revenue, as an example, generated in 2015, increasing to $132.57 billion in 2020, attaining a compound annual growth rate (CAGR) of 9.14%.*

The SaaS idea such as saleforce.com came out as early as in 1999, which since then started to forge a groundbreaking model in the field of enterprise software applications such as from Amazon Web Services, Office 365, and ERP. Together with Infrastructure as a Service (IaaS), Platform as a Service (PaaS), SaaS moves applications to the Cloud, making them widely available for organizations of all shapes and sizes, allowing end users to access applications from anywhere, using a web-enabled device.

Such a trend has also caused businesses to think differently when deploying long distance networks, or WANs, as traditional technologies like MPLS were not built for the Cloud. Meanwhile customers at every level expect the delivery of Cloud services with the same level of quality that traditional MPLS networks offered in years past. To experience the full power of the Cloud, the users need seamless connectivity that is flexible and dynamic across all domains. Without a reliable link to the Cloud, there will be literally no effective IaaS, PaaS, or SaaS and the explosive productivity they bring onboard.

Legacy managed WAN bandwidth like MPLS was so fixed and expensive that often enterprises find it difficult to manage an effective network performance. For peak use, they have to either overbuild the network to account or reconfigure it in short notice with a costly and highly manual solution. With regard to new provisioning and changes, the networking team then had to manually configure and roll out proprietary routers to the branch and create a hub-and-spoke architecture.

Some enterprises, on the other hand, have tried out "dummy" public Internet for internal Cloud links but the links can be unreliable and slow, due to heavy traffic, packet loss, and fluctuating latencies.

* EMA Report: Digital Transformation Demands a Next-Generation Wide-Area Network released in December 2016.

Application slowness results in poor worker experience which negatively impacts productivity.

Now comes SD-WAN that makes a big difference with more values added: It can connect branches to the head office by transforming the network into an open and programmable Cloud infrastructure. Replacing the traditional hub-and-spoke model, it can deploy a partial or fully meshed architecture and transport traffic along the most efficient path. Customers will no longer pay a premium for high-reliability, low-latency, secure MPLS links because SD-WAN can help solve these challenges while traversing the public Internet links.

A Use Case: SD-WAN Cloud Connection

Hudson Finance Inc. is a firm handling private equity and stock trading for a large base of clients. Since they've moved many applications to the Cloud, recently they switched to an SD-WAN Cloud connection for the HQ and each of their 75 branches across the country. Their service provider came and deployed an SD-WAN box or vCPE on each of their sites, and the vCPE sends their traffic to a Cloud gateway, which then connects the client to their Cloud applications and keeps their Cloud sessions running.

The SD-WAN provider that Hudson Finance signed on has direct connections to the major Cloud service providers. This means once the Hudson's traffic hits the SD-WAN provider's nearest Cloud gateway, it will get connected directly to the Cloud providers with no need to continue traversing the public Internet to reach the Cloud destinations. This means less latency, packet loss, and jitter which equates to a better user experience with the Hudson's Cloud applications.

The SD-WAN connection would also do automatic load balancing and instant fail over to a better circuit when needed. For instance, teams in Hudson Finance from time to time use hosted video conferencing from different locations in a conference session, when if suddenly the primary Internet connection got lost, the group will not lose their meeting because the Cloud gateway keeps the session constant while it reconnects to the client's site's secondary Internet connection, within milliseconds.

Cost-saving wise, Hudson used to pay seven times more for MPLS connectivity for all their sites and got locked up with a single service

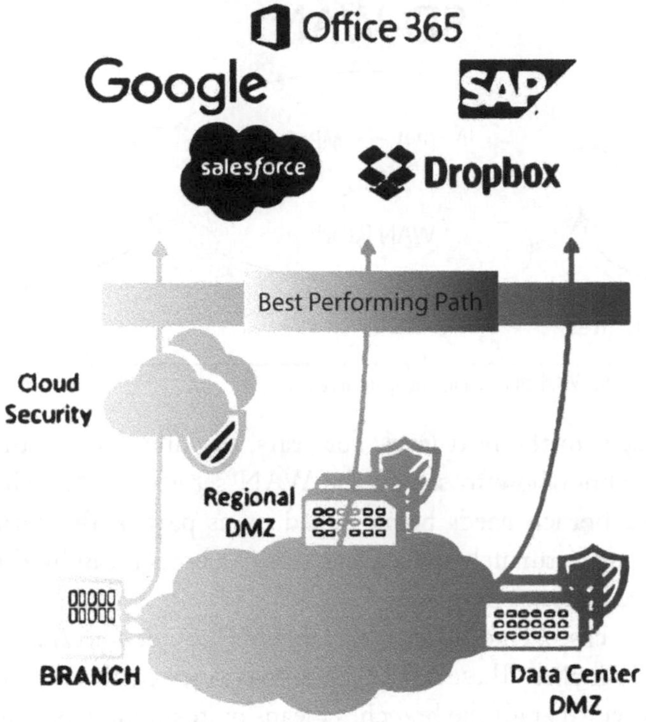

Figure 2.3 Direct connectivity to Cloud-based software applications.

provider for years. Their realization that the service provider was less motivated to improve their WAN technologies for the concern of revenue erosion, actually prompted Hudson to make their mind to try out SD-WAN and eventually stay with it (Figure 2.3).

Simplifying and Boosting Branches & SMBs

> SD-WAN makes it very easy to augment more bandwidth at each branch by using a second broadband circuit to supplement the existing MPLS link, or completely replacing the MPLS circuit with dual high-bandwidth broadband circuits.

SD-WAN is enabling new branch office WAN models as illustrated in Figure 2.4. As companies continue to rely upon apps and services from the Cloud and data centers, the branch infrastructure needs

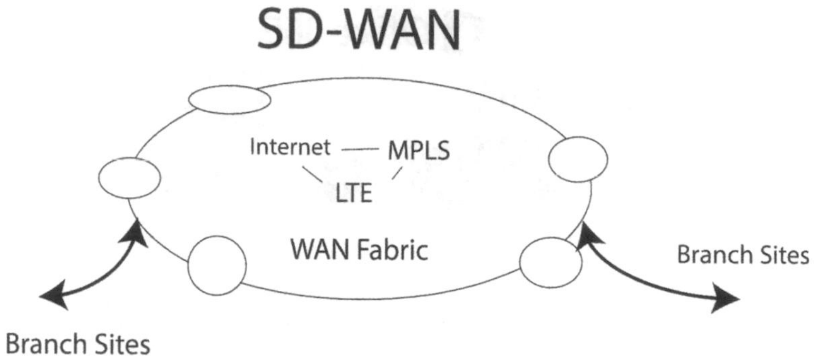

Figure 2.4 SD-WAN simplifying branch operations.

being taken to the next level. For years, the dilemma for the enterprises is about how to set up the WAN service for branch offices: while the branch needs being linked up as part of the corporation network, unfortunately the average size of a branch can hardly justify the high cost for such links.

In most cases, enterprises use a large MPLS network that connects all their branches. These MPLS circuits are very costly and increasing the bandwidth at all the branches means quite an incremental spending on the WAN. On the other hand, the regular public Internet and IPsec VPN can't handle an enterprise traffic in terms of reliability, security, and quality.

Hence, one of the top reasons to deploy SD-WAN is to increase bandwidth at the branches at a better cost. SD-WAN makes it very easy to augment more bandwidth at each branch by using a second broadband circuit for non-critical traffic to supplement the existing MPLS circuit for critical traffic, or completely replacing the MPLS circuit with dual high-bandwidth broadband circuits. This makes adding more bandwidth more effective while reducing the cost at the same time.

Deploying vCPEs and replacing old hardware at the branches could be another benefit. If equipment is old and misses some new functionalities, then deploying SD-WAN will provide opportunities for more innovation at the branch. vCPEs that blend the new SDN/NFV capabilities will replace the regular CPEs that have little future for the business growth.

SD-WAN is also good news for small and medium businesses (SMBs) who are in need of WAN solutions especially like direct high-speed Cloud links but cannot afford legacy WAN solutions like MPLS in setup, operation, and maintenance. An SD-WAN would be SMBs' best option to lower costs and offer the most competitive level of services.

A Use Case: Branch Optimization for DTS Technologies

DTS Technologies, Inc. is an engineering consulting and construction company based in Denver, Colorado. Currently it has dozens of branch offices and remote sites from 30 to 1 personnel range throughout the West Coast and Mountain Area, using a mix of access like MPLS, dedicated T1, DSL, and satellite to connect to the corporate WAN.

In recent years, the firm has migrated some major servers to be hosted from the Cloud and employees are supposed to run their daily work via software apps from the Cloud as well. Also, engineering designing and consulting often requires audio and video conferencing and file sharing either internally with the team or externally with the client but transferring large files plus real time could result in high traffic bottleneck, bandwidth consumption, and poor performance.

Such disparate technologies and connections make their WAN very tough to manage, and the firm's small IT team often spent a long time to cope with users and the service providers associated on trouble shooting for latency, device issues, security concern, network management, and visibility issues. As the result both direct and hidden cost of running the current WAN has gone out of control.

Couple of years ago, the firm has tackled the possibility to have a service provider come in and set up MPLS connections for the corporate WAN, but eventually gave it up due to high cost and long provisioning cycle.

After some intense exploration in late 2016, DTS finally decided to choose a managed SD-WAN for an overall WAN upgrading which delivers a true Cloud-like operating model for the firm including all the branches. The initiation setup for the SD-WAN solution only took five working days to complete: the SD-WAN vendor instantly provisions new branches by drop-shipping low-cost, white-box hardware like standard x86 systems populated with software that is auto-provisioned to predefined templates.

On the Cloud end, the service provider easily routes the traffic to their gateways deployed in Cloud data centers nationally, where all applications and workloads are delivered via the most optimized data paths to the users.

For DTS, SD-WAN means dramatic cost savings, more reliability over the WAN environment, from bandwidth to security to high performance, and fast new provisioning and troubleshooting when needed. Now their small IT staff can focus more on productivity and strategic coordination with business requirements.

Enhancing WAN Cybersecurity

SD-WAN has an upper hand in cybersecurity management and can bring up more enhanced and cost-effective security measures and defense for enterprises, especially for their formerly vulnerable branch offices.

According to the report from IHS Markit issued in November 2017,* the number of reported major cyber-attacks recently doubled in just 1 year, from 80,000 in 2016 to nearly 160,000 in 2017. Network operators have been seeing hundreds of thousands of botnet threats each day.

Human beings often have to face dilemmas. One good example is from the modern IT and network communication arena. On one hand, we keep innovating the ways we connect and communicate to each other; on the other hand, the more open and software driven the network becomes, the more likely it will face security threat and breaches.

One hot segment is in application security, driven by the exponential growth of the IoT and corporate "bring your own device" policies. This is because traditionally the ingress/egress points in a network were mostly limited to the enterprises' offices, buildings, or data centers. But today, partner connections across Intranet and even the boarders, consumer and employee mobile devices, and more direct Internet access from branches have significantly increased the number of attack points in a network and made it very hard to defend.

---

* Wide Area Networking (WAN) Strategies North American Enterprise Survey-2017.

Figure 2.5 Cybersecurity.

Hence, the need for reliable, secure, and high-performance WAN and Internet connectivity has never been greater (as illustrated by Figure 2.5). SD-WAN has an upper hand in cybersecurity management. With the budget constraints nowadays in funding growing WAN bandwidth consumption, more companies are planning to deploy SD-WAN with more robust security capabilities to better control how their WANs are used.

SD-WAN can bring up more enhanced and cost-effective security measures and defense for enterprises, especially for their formerly vulnerable branch offices. In the past, to deploy robust security in branch offices was either too costly to do or too hard to manage, security solutions like firewall, DNS security, and web gateway security might each need a separate box for configuration, installation, and management.

But now SD-WAN can bundle and enhance all these security solutions via remotely centralized, policy-based software intelligence and then push the security solutions through to each of the enterprises' branches.

For instance, Versa Networks—an SD-WAN startup HQed in Silicon Valley, CA, has launched its FlexVNF software-defined security products, covering DNS security and a secure Web gateway. Both are key for smooth and secure Internet access services.

DNS security protects against phishing, botnet access, and advanced persistent threats (APT), and augments reputation systems with zero-day validation of domains. Secure Web gateway performs SSL encryption/decryption and granular URL filtering, and integrates with other Versa security functions for layered user group policies, file filtering, IP filtering, and DNS mapping.

Service deployment and management wise, it will take much less time to set up the SDN/NFV based security services via vCPEs, and also make the security management ongoing basis more agile and scalable.

Since the hackers never stop coming up with new tricks and malware, SD-WAN can be more responsive to such new types of cyberattacks and plots so as to target and thwart them.

One big advantage is SD-WAN offers a holistic visibility into the amount and types of traffic traversing the network. Any kind of anomaly can instantly flag on a security issue or something that draws the administrator's attention. Plus the big data capability of SD-WAN through the Cloud would also make security threats and their pattern tracking, analyzing, info sharing, and reporting more effective.

Some pessimists view network security is a losing battle. It is not, but it won't be a quick win either. Instead it would be a protracted war. Again, the biggest challenge is as our network services grow and expand, so do the security threats.

The key is when deploying an SD-WAN solution, always keep the security elements in mind. SD-WAN is not just for cost saving and service agility, it is about network security as well. Only when well-planned and well-managed, SD-WAN can become a win–win for both the network service providers and their enterprise end users.

SD-WAN Buying Criteria and Vendor Selection

> The following nine criteria can typically be used in assessing and selecting an SD-WAN solution or vendor.

With SD-WAN becoming more popular in the WAN infrastructure marketplace, questions from enterprises arise that there are dozens of SD-WAN vendors out there, which one would make our best choice?

Most SD-WAN experts or consultants would answer it depends on the enterprise's specific needs and situation. Then an enterprise may

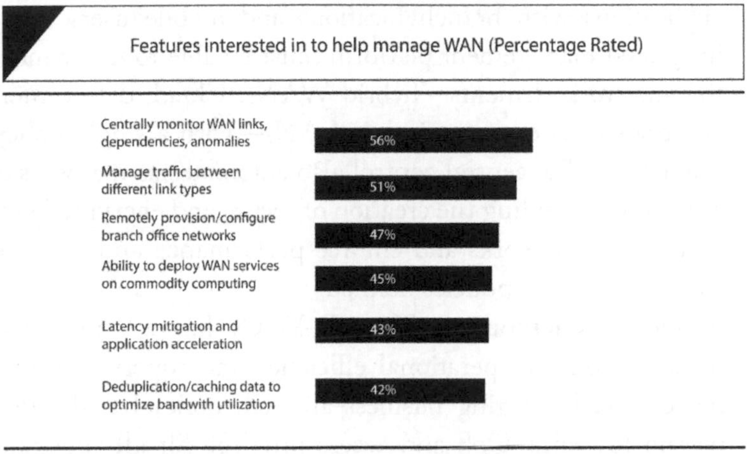

Figure 2.6 WAN selection criteria.

Source: **Forrester, survey of U.S Network and Telecom Decision Makers.**

follow, "I know my needs, but how do I match an SD-WAN vendor's strengths with my needs?"

Compared to the general WAN selection criteria as illustrated in Figure 2.6, the following nine criteria can typically be used in assessing and selecting an SD-WAN solution or vendor. When assessing SD-WAN, it's important to weigh individual features and benefits against the broader capabilities as suggested by the Business Case ROI described at the start of this chapter, make sure that the offering must deliver to fulfill the promise of reduced complexity, better speed, and performance.

1. **Innovative and Converged Solution:** SD-WAN solutions provide a lightweight replacement for traditional WAN routers and are agnostic to WAN transport technologies, that is, they support MPLS, Internet, Long Term Evolution [LTE], etc.
2. **Network Multiplexing and Load Balancing:** SD-WAN combines multiple physical circuits into a logical network, so there is no connection conflict impeding access for other devices. Check support for load balancing schemes offered (active/active being the most notable), tunnel bonding, and failover times between connections.
3. **Central Management:** SD-WAN offers a single-pane view into the fabric that connects the data center and the Cloud

applications with branch locations and mobile users. That integrated management platform must be able to unify multiple network elements—hybrid WANs, Cloud, data center, and branch wired and wireless LANs—with a single policy framework. The central control also automates as many tasks as possible including the creation of secure and encrypted virtual private networks and enforce performance and security controls based on policies defined.

4. **Service Orchestration:** The SD-WAN has a centralized orchestration for operational efficiency and superior performance, via leveraging business-aligned, policy-based automation to define QoS and access privilege for all apps and users. The orchestration should ensure automated and secure connections between Cloud networks and branch networks and provide seamless integration with all network services.
5. **Path Selection:** SD-WANs should be able to monitor the characteristics of the various paths to between two locations, selecting the optimum path for a given application. How this is done relies on a number of features including the criteria monitored by the SD-WAN (latency, packet loss, and jitter are most common) and whether the SD-WAN can select from paths or physical connections.
6. **Agility:** Rapid deployment is the hallmark of an SD-WAN. SD-WAN should support zero-touch deployment at a minimum. In today's highly distributed enterprise, branch offices are often essential to the enterprise. To achieve the agility and efficiency that business demands, the SD-WAN solution should provide the capability to provision new branch equipment quickly and remotely without sending a technician to set up the network.
7. **Resiliency:** Look for redundancy and failover throughout the SD-WAN. SD-WAN nodes, for example, should be able to sit out-of-path and SD-WAN controllers should be redundant. Evaluate SD-WAN behavior in the event of a link failure, brownout, or blackout. With SD-WAN services, the network core should be fully redundant with customers being automatically connected to the next closest point-of-presence (PoP) in the event of an outage.

8. **Security:** All SD-WANs should offer encrypted tunnels and most offer basic firewalling. But a secure SD-WAN goes a step further and incorporates advanced security, such as a next-generation firewall and anti-malware. This is particularly important in the branch office.
9. **Management and Visibility:** Steering traffic depends on being able to accurately classify traffic. SD-WAN providers should detail how they classify applications, the parameters that can be configured for application profiles, and the kinds of dashboards and reporting around application usage and performance.

A Closer Look at SD-WAN Vendors

> These sale results may allow us to further differentiate the SD-WAN vendors, because the market would favor certain vendors for a reason.

Nowadays we see most SD-WAN vendors carry the capabilities and solutions associated along the guidelines above. What additional criteria or qualifications can be used for enterprises to scan and vet the SD-WAN landscape, so as to pin down the vendor in need?

We may draw some inspiration from the quarterly IHS Market Report* which shows the right business focus makes a difference in the highly innovative and competitive SD-WAN market. Based on the report, the second quarter of 2017 brought in a total revenue of $78 million in SD-WAN market, indicating a robust increase of 33% compared to $58.7 million for the first quarter of the same year.

According to this report, these vendors hold tight the top three seats in SD-WAN sales: VeloCloud, Viptela, and Talari Networks. The only difference is for the first quarter of the same year, Viptela was in the first place with $7.7 million revenue and VeloCloud as the second with $4.9 million; however, by the second quarter VeloCloud

* IHS Markit Data Center Network Equipment Quarterly Market Tracker report issued in July and September 2017.

surged to $24 million and grabbed away the first place, even though Viptela also grew to $9.2 million.

These sale results may allow us to further differentiate the SD-WAN vendors, because the market would favor certain vendors for a reason. We can label VeloCloud (in November 2017 it was acquired by VMWare) as a "Cloud Access Builder"; Viptela and Talari as "MPLS/Cisco Rivals" (Viptela now is acquired by Cisco); Versa Networks as a "Branch Networks Virtualizer"; Silver Peak and Riverbed as "Network Optimizing Doctors"; and Cisco's iWAN as a "Transitional WAN Player."

VeloCloud has been positioning itself as "the cloud-delivered SD-WAN company," which recently reached a new milestone with 50 Tier-1 and Tier-2 service provider partners, in addition to 1,000 enterprise customers for its SD-WAN platform. It looks like their strategic focus on Cloud WAN access and architecture, which strikes head on a major pain point that most enterprises are facing today, is paying back.

Next-gen Cloud access and performance requires high bandwidth, low latency and jitter, cost-effective, and secured connectivity network, while the hub–and-spoke structured MPLS cannot handle such Cloud access and performance well. Thus, VeloCloud can come to the enterprises with an appealing pitch: We will re-align your network topology and directly link your company, especially the branch offices, to the Cloud for virtual data center and SaaS applications, by providing a transport independent secure overlay enabling the use of broadband Internet with or without traditional MPLS, and a business-driven orchestration layer for automation and virtual services insertion.

This is not saying other vendors like Viptela, Talari, Silver Peak, Riverbed, and so on cannot link enterprise to the Cloud. Surely they can and actually Cloud direct access plays a key part of the SD-WAN portfolio they offer as well. But their business positioning on the Cloud is relatively murky and the focus is not as sharp as VeloCloud's towards Cloud service integration.

In August 2017, VeloCloud announced the expansion of its Security Technology Partner Program, allowing enterprises to choose and use security solution providers they've already worked with or favor. This reveals the goal that the firm is determined to establish a Cloud powered SD-WAN ecosystem.

Viptela and Talari seem to plan on being an alternative or even replacement to the legacy MPLS, especially Cisco powered MPLS networks. No blame is on them for such positioning because the original SD-WAN concept came up to disrupt the MPLS mainstream WAN solutions. But realistically we have to admit for an MPLS centric enterprise to adopt and transition to SD-WAN, it will take time to happen. Key factors like existing network architecture, sunk-in facilities, resource availability, organization impact, security, and compliance considerations can all be barriers in the road.

Comparatively VeloCloud's approach sends a cozier message to the enterprises about their very needed Cloud access, as either a supplement or alternative to the legacy MPLS or DSL. This may make the enterprise internal decision-making process easier, for instance, the IT Dept. can stress to their C-level more the SD-WAN's benefits of direct and cost-effective Cloud access, rather than hitting the sensitive MPLS re-shuffling topics.

Versa Networks, on the other hand, with a strong background of Network Functions Virtualization (NFV), has been targeting the carrier and managed service providers (MSP) for simplifying the branch office WAN solutions for enterprises. For example, Versa can virtualize and centralize multiple network functions over one single "white box" as a router, a VPN concentrator, a stateful firewall, a network address translator, an intrusion prevention system, and other functions.

For vendors like Silver Peak and Riverbed, their network optimization background has some tradeoffs in today's market. The pro is they can take advantage their existing customer base and convert the services to SD-WAN. The con is new clients may have questions or suspicions about if their SD-WAN solution is full-fledged and competitive enough or just some quick re-branding from their hardware-based network optimization package. It might take some due marketing diligence to change their images from network flowing doctors to next-gen WAN infrastructure experts.

For international SD-WAN solutions, since the public Internet backbone becomes harder to manage as a performance reliable and consistent underlay, some companies, with Aryaka as an example, have chosen to build private Clouds or networks to reduce the variability in response times. Aryaka runs its SD-WAN over a private network by leasing Layer 2 connectivity from Tier-1 networks globally with access to 95% of the Points of Presence (PoPs) used by business customers. The book will provide more elaboration on Aryaka's business case in Chapter III.

Furthermore, Cisco's iWAN, although only a partial SD-WAN solution, can fit those enterprise who already installed many Cisco devices and are still in the middle of the service life-cycle. iWAN can be taken as a spin-off from Cisco's internal SDN and NFV reforms to simplify network devices, centralize the control, and become more cost-effective. Ongoing basis, since now Cisco has bought over Viptela, it clearly indicates the ramp-up as iWAN's replacement.

SD-WAN Solution and Deployment Models

> Today there are basically three types of WAN solution models: Dual MPLS, hybrid of MPLS, and Internet or dual Internet.

If an enterprise needs WAN services, what is the best model of solution to go after?

Today there are basically three types of WAN solution models: Dual MPLS, hybrid of MPLS, and Internet or dual Internet, as illustrated in Figure 2.7. MPLS is the legacy model, while the hybrid and dual Internet models represent the trend. To reach 99.999% network availability, any SD-WAN solution combination should be able to do

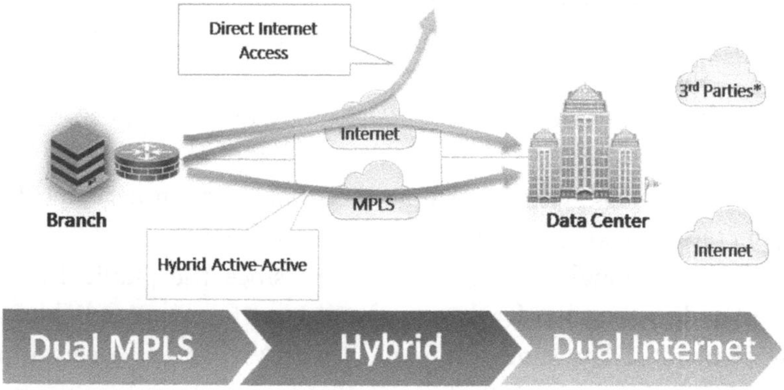

Figure 2.7 WAN solution models.

active/active load balancing; fast session/packet failover, and detect blackout/brownout.

To ensure a successful SD-WAN solution, the first step is quite the same with the Business Case process discussed at the start of this chapter, that is to identify network requirements, needs, and the expected costs associated. Then assess and determine the performance metrics, security and management protocols of the WAN accordingly.

Based on the networking need and requirement, the enterprise decides on what deployment models to take on. For instance, the hybrid model would be a transitional approach, while cutting the MPLS cord and replacing it with dual Internet link is kind of an aggressive move.

Meanwhile, make sure the solution chosen does not disrupt existing communication and IT operations, and that the changeover is as seamless as possible. Major installation and service cutover should happen in non-work or off-peak hours. This is the convergence topic we will discuss further below. By the way, although SD-WAN can handle network security quite effectively and in a fine-tuned manner, the IT staff may want to take some new training to better understand and take advantage of SD-WAN's security capabilities.

Finally, it's always a smart idea to conduct pilots and testing on SD-WAN. The approach provides the tryout of an SD-WAN solution for like 90 days for free, which allows companies to discover and work through any problems and then make future deployments easier. The pilot testing, adjusting, and modifying will help consolidate the official rollout procedure. Also, phased deployment from metro, regional, national, and international sites is recommended to guarantee the success of SD-WAN adoption.

The Popular Hybrid Solution

Hybrid SD-WAN is expected to lead the solution model.

As SD-WAN adoption continues to gain ground and go mainstream in the next 2 or 3 years, hybrid SD-WAN is expected to lead the solution model, meaning the majority of initial enterprise deployments will be hybrid, leveraging both MPLS and a complement overlay of broadband connectivity.

Here is the main reason: many enterprises already have some level of broadband connectivity to branch and remote locations, but these links often remain idle or are relegated to backup or disaster recovery. What the enterprises will begin to do is to downgrade the MPLS subscription and lower the cost, meanwhile fully leverage the broadband Internet link for an SD-WAN overlay to scale bandwidth cost-effectively in line with expanding application and user requirements.

As already stated in many occasions in this book, legacy MPLS has shortfalls such as long deployment timelines, high cost, and lack of optimized Cloud access support, while an SD-WAN overlay can greatly reduce the shortfalls of conventional public Internet in terms of slow and unreliable application performance due to high packet loss, fluctuating latencies, and easy security breaches.

Deploying a hybrid SD-WAN solution then becomes a realistic and flexible choice to mitigate the disadvantages of regular MPLS and public Internet WAN connections, giving enterprises the capabilities of both a Cloud only and site to site design in a meshing VPN topology. The hybrid model brings about local edge devices that are application-aware and make routing decisions based on the end destination of the packet and the priority assigned. This gives businesses the flexibility of routing to either Cloud or premise-based application, using SD-WAN intelligence.

The advantages of the hybrid model are obvious, but a caveat is it remains a "half SD-WAN," meaning the MPLS and Internet underlay are still inherently in the old platform, thus it is more complex to set up and converge than a Cloud only solution and provides less robust security features than a premise-based solution. This can lead to a challenge with network configuration in mixing an existing premise firewall with implementing a Cloud-based security platform.

If the same hybrid model is duplicated to new sites, then the slow MPLS provisioning part may still drags the leg of service readiness timeline. Still some enterprise may want to keep an MPLS circuit on existing and new sites for mission critical or highly regulated data traffic.

Three Approaches of SD-WAN Deployment

There are three key criteria for your consideration when selecting an SD-WAN deployment approach: cost, integration, and features & capabilities.

If your organization has learnt about SD-WAN and its benefits and now is thinking seriously on its deployment, then what major options are there on the table that you can pick?

Fundamentally there are three options for SD-WAN deployment: Do it yourself (DIY), purchase it from a managed service provider, or make it a hybrid deployment. Some large enterprises who have sufficient internal IT and networking resources may still prefer to install and manage the services by themselves.

Mid- and small-size businesses and organizations, on the other hand, are more likely to take on a managed SD-WAN solution from a service provider, or a hybrid deployment that splits the control between the service provider and end user.

Here we can do some deep diving into this managed SD-WAN service model (as shown in Figure 2.8, including the hybrid flavor), because the end user will again face three options of source: pure play SD-WAN providers, WAN optimization and virtualization vendors, or telecom carriers and cable operators.

Several pure play SD-WAN providers, such as CloudGenix, VeloCloud (being acquired by VMWare), Viptela (being acquired by

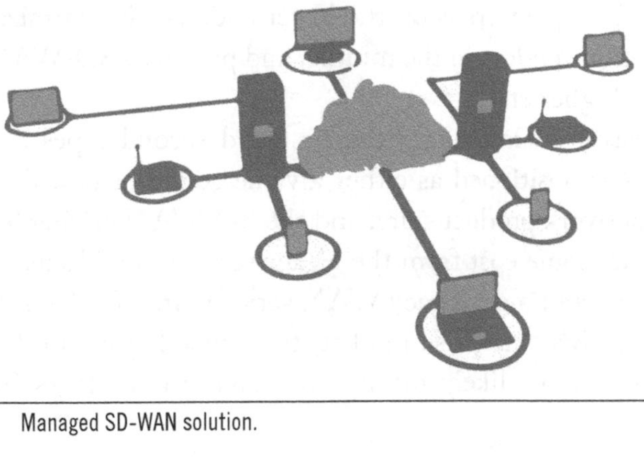

Figure 2.8 Managed SD-WAN solution.

Cisco), and Versa, have emerged from the Silicon Valley and effectively developed and provisioned SD-WAN solutions. Their original solutions, with little legacy service constraints, can deliver flexible network agnostic SD-WAN overlay, high speed and direct Cloud connectivity, and high degrees of operational efficiencies via central policy controllers.

Some WAN optimization and virtualization vendors, such as Citrix, Silver Peak, Riverbed, FatPipe Networks, Talari Networks, and Ecessa have moved into the SD-WAN space via a value-added approach. They also offer SD-WAN overlay solutions, rich application policy management, and operational efficiencies via central policy controllers.

Several telecom carriers and cable operators (such as Verizon, AT&T, BT, Orange Business Services, CenturyLink, China Telecom Global, Windstream, Comcast, Charter, etc.) have launched managed SD-WAN services. In most cases the SD-WAN is part of their national or global WAN service portfolio, which provides the mix of SD-WAN as well as traditional solutions such as MPLS or dedicated private lines.

Hence when facing the above offers of SD-WAN deployment, how can your organization make a sound choice?

There are three key criteria for your consideration when selecting an SD-WAN deployment approach: cost, integration, and features & capabilities.

Based on various assessments to date, SD-WAN is poised to save 30%–80% of service cost compared to legacy WAN solutions like MPLS. Across this 30%–80% saving span, we can say telecom carriers and cable operators is on the lower end, WAN optimization and virtualization vendors in the middle, and pure play SD-WAN providers on the higher end.

The reason is simple, for the first and second types of vendors, SD-WAN is positioned as either a value added or new line to their existing network product suite, and the SD-WAN pricing has to burden or share some cost from the legacy service side. As technology is fast evolving and most legacy WAN services are in a flat or declining mode in today's enterprise market, the general cost base from these vendors will most likely offset some saving advantages SD-WAN brings about.

The pure play providers, on the other hand, only focus on the SD-WAN solution via a network agnostic overlay and Cloud-based architecture, without any legacy constraints and mix to worry about, and therefore can often maximize the cost saving in their SD-WAN offer to the end users. Based on my firm's best practice of SD-WAN deployment over these couple of years, if for example cost savings and direct connectivity of Cloud applications are the major objectives of your organization in adopting SD-WAN, then a pure play provider can easily stand out in the candidate short list.

Integration means if you are already a customer of some WAN optimization and virtualization vendor, or telecom carrier and cable operator, and now they've launched SD-WAN as well, then the situation may be an easy "ramp-up" for both sides.

Unless you feel to revamp your WAN service for cost savings or lose confidence in continuing on with the traditional services, picking the incumbent vendor's offer usually makes a smooth integration between the SD-WAN and existing network services you've signed up there. Some pure play providers may not be that experienced in orchestrating and synchronizing such integrations.

Features & capabilities are no doubt critical for organizations in picking an SD-WAN solution. While most SD-WAN solutions offer good cost savings, fast provisioning, better Cloud links, simpler branch operation, optimized service control, and security, some clients may look for an SD-WAN package with certain special features such as integration with VoIP, WAN optimization service, advanced security enhancement, IoT, big data and AI capabilities, etc. In such cases, those SD-WAN vendors who can meet these special requirements become more favorable during the selection process.

As for the hybrid approach of the managed SD-WAN services, again it's mostly about the degrees of control between the services provider and end user. In some cases, some end users, while letting the service provider dealing with anything related to the core network operation and maintenance, may want to handle some "edge customizations" like new site and link expansion, compliance rules, and application access policy on their own. Those vendors who can offer such customized controls to the end users will differentiate themselves from other competitors.

In a nutshell, the right deployment approach or strategy makes a pivotal step in SD-WAN service adoption. Some organizations are also attempting the multi-vendor approach in hope of maximizing the SD-WAN benefits, like for the existing network services they go with the SD-WAN offer from the current telecom carrier, while for some new and global sites expansion, they sign on with a pure play SD-WAN provider.

Monitoring and Managing SD-WAN Performance

SD-WAN provides a great interactive and intelligent platform with powerful tools for easy monitoring and traffic management of WAN transport, security, and interoperability with other WAN elements.

The SD-WAN service provider typically offers portals, platforms, and tested practices and processes to enable the client to implement SD-WAN with confidence. The Managed SD-WAN service portal (see, e.g., Figure 2.9) would provide the tools, monitoring, oversight, and life-cycle support for the end user to maintain application visibility and control.

By leveraging a professional portal and platform supplied by the service provider, clients can absorb the new technology into their organization without making drastic changes, which can improve the efficiency of the client network and communications. The service provider's life-cycle management approach can help clients develop a migration plan that suits their readiness now and in the future.

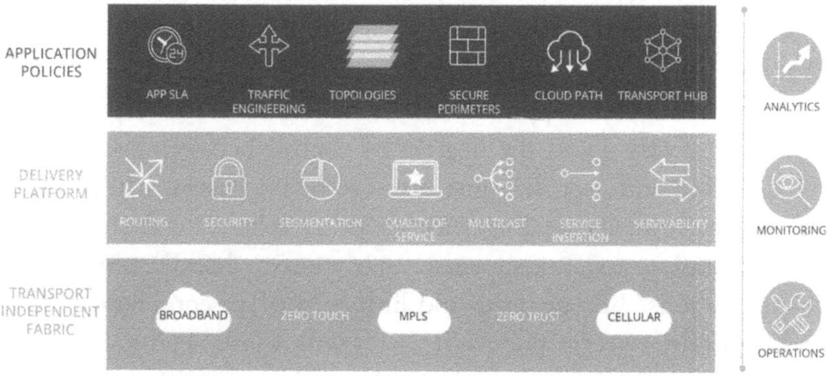

Figure 2.9 SD-WAN management portal.

In daily operations, most clients use the graphical Management Console or Portal provided by the SD-WAN supplier to help manage traffic and application QoS. The console is capable to manage traffic types ranging from ERP to voice and video, plus other features like security requirements, user location, and application location—whether the application is hosted in the data center or in the Cloud.

Clients can also sue the SD-WAN service portal tackling platform convergence at the finger tips, managing multiple QoS for different applications, multiple access technologies, multiple router, switch and CPEs, and security methodologies over a single platform.

A Use Case of SD-WAN Performance Management

The IT staff of St. Thomas Hospital recently got trained on how to use the SD-WAN service portal after the hospital decided to adopt SD-WAN for its WAN and Cloud access of similar quality to MPLS but at a lower cost.

St. Thomas Hospital uses two or more WAN connectivity types such as MPLS, SD-WAN overlay on broadband Internet, and 4G LTE. The IT staff depends on the management portal to integrate and track the reliability and performance of certain links from specific service providers, i.e., adjusting traffic patterns when application performance suffers. The central control also allows the hospital to unify SD-WAN and branch router management to simplify operations, such as supporting legacy routing protocols configuration like BGP to facilitate management of MPLS links.

The hospital's IT team is taking advantage of the SD-WAN Management Portal in terms of:

- Accessing reports on path quality, application prioritization, utilization, trending, and changes in application path selection
- Fault/configuration/change management of the underlying hybrid platform and transport services
- Instrumentation of path quality and management of associated thresholds and alarms. Proactive traffic management with refreshing application rules and path selection

- Troubleshooting performance issues—prioritizing the hospital's communications in the case of a bandwidth limitation, so that network traffic related to certain applications line data server for Emergency Care has a higher priority than those related to some non-critical data flow.

For service security, the hospital used to be lack of transparency when leveraging third-party security organizations for architecting and deploying security technologies, such as firewalls and unified threat management at branch locations to help protect their WAN traffic.

Now the hospital's IT staff can use SD-WAN central management portal to seamlessly interoperate with branch, data center, and Cloud-based security with security vendor partners, uncovering, identifying, and mitigating security risks in real time.

3
Launch of SD-WAN Service

A Conversation with the VP of a Telco

> Our goal is to increase our addressable opportunities and provide businesses with an innovation as they migrate from legacy technologies.

As more and more communication service providers (CSPs) such as telecom carriers, cable service operators, and managed service providers (MSPs) are debuting SD-WAN solutions to the enterprise market, recently I found a chance to sit down with a vice president of a US telecom carrier during a trade show and had a discussion on their SD-WAN offer and how it has impacted their business and customers.

Author (A): Thanks for taking time to have this conversation on SD-WAN.

Vice President (V): My pleasure. Quite an exciting time to talk about SD-WAN.

A: Great. When did your firm launch SD-WAN as a product?

V: Around the 3rd quarter of 2016. The goal is to increase our addressable opportunities and provide businesses with an innovation as they migrate from legacy technologies.

A: What do you see driving your SD-WAN rollout to the market?

V: We see today's IT environment for enterprises is quickly evolving and demands some new WAN services to handle a growing number of users accessing the network from a wide array of locations with widely varying access options. For instance, Cloud-based enterprise applications. As WAN management has become more challenging and resource intensive, SD-WAN emerges as an effective solution.

A: What does your SD-WAN package offer?

V: From high level, these three main features. Transport Overlay: Featuring built-in load balancing and automatic fail-over capability, agnostic to the underlay hybrid links of MPLS, public Internet, and LTE cellular. Central Orchestration: Centralized network visibility and control, as well as QoS and bandwidth management with traffic shaping. Policy-based routing: Assigns a traffic path based on source, destination or application; and dynamic path selection, which chooses a traffic path per-application based on loss, latency, and jitter.

A: Sounds quite standard. Any optional services offered as well?

V: On top of the standard IPsec feature for our SD-WAN security, upon client's request, we can also offer enhanced security package as optional such as secure connectivity with AES encryption, PCI/DSS, IDS/IPS, web filtering, etc.

A: I've heard that some carriers who have MPLS as existing WAN solutions may have concerns that SD-WAN may cannibalize the lucrative revenue from MPLS.

V: Well, there are some tradeoffs. Here's our take on this matter: first we can regard SD-WAN as an opportunity to acquire new revenue streams and provide a better experience for the customer base, all while keeping pace with the transforming enterprise networking market. If we don't do it while others are doing, it would only put us at a disadvantage. Guess this is the so-called Effect of Competition.

A: True. The competition always drives the market reforms.

V: Second, nearly every technology upgrade or innovation causes some loss of revenue from the existing solutions. When MPLS replaced frame relay and ATM about 15 years ago, same revenue erosion concern existed. But we can only go with this flow that nowadays customers intend to pay less for doing more. What we can do for revenue growth is to keep adding values to the new products and expanding the market.

A: How do you use SD-WAN to enhance your WAN product portfolio?

V: One big thing we've done is to position SD-WAN as a supplement rather than replacement to MPLS. We don't encourage clients especially with long-haul data traffic to completely terminate the existing MPLS service, not just for our sake of the revenue protection of MPLS, rather from a class of service, reliability, and availability perspectives. MPLS is still valuable to the enterprises although its weight and proportion in the total WAN solution can be reduced somehow because of the emerging SD-WAN solution. That's why we offer a hybrid portfolio to our enterprise market and it proves to be quite successful so far.

A: Glad to know your hybrid approach works. How did you start with SD-WAN? Internally or partnering with an external partner?

V: We've started to implement SDN/NVF internally since 2012–2013 timeframe with the goal to simplifying the network operation, increase provisioning efficiencies, and reducing service costs. After couple of years we realized SDN/NFV can be offered such as SD-WAN to our enterprise market as a next-gen service choice beyond MPLS.

A: So, you have an in-house team to develop your SD-WAN offer?

V: Actually no. Our in-house team is more on the internal network engineering and NOC side to manage, monitor troubleshoot, and maintain the network. We teamed up with an SD-WAN solution developer in Silicon Valley to roll out the service.

A: What were the typical market reactions when you initiated the SD-WAN launch?

V: Many clients showed great interest, especially in the expected savings by reducing reliance on costly MPLS connections, but wanted to see some proof of concept first, especially from network reliability, agility, and security standpoints. So, we ran a lot of workshop and demos, and also offered a 90-days free trial program to the market.

A: What about the pricing for SD-WAN? Are customers concerned with some initial setup fee for SD-WAN?

V: Well, we've tried to address any pricing concern from a 1–2-year long-term ROI perspectives. It really depends on the customer situation. For example, some clients at start just need SD-WAN for direct Cloud application links. Then they can start to downgrade their MPLS connections and use SD-WAN instead. Such services should produce immediate savings to the client with little initiation cost

A: At what scenarios customers may not see savings immediately?

V: That's when the client adopts the SD-WAN as a complete hybrid solution and as the result has to reshuffle their network architecture, security set up, even organization changes, etc. They may see some initial cost of doing such but in long term the SD-WAN service would surely pay back.

A: What requirements did you put up when picking up the SD-WAN partner?

V: That's a good question. First and foremost, we really want a so-called "pure player" of SD-WAN developer. Namely they need to stay away from the incumbent network hardware and devices and put up an agnostic Cloud-based overlay for SD-WAN. This would allow us to differentiate with MPLS solution to our customers as much possible.

A: You mean you don't pick something like the Cisco iWAN solution that is still tied to the existing routers, switches, and accelerators in the network, etc.

V: We work closely with Cisco on legacy solutions. But we need SD-WAN as a Cloud-based overlay on top the client's existing network infrastructure like MPLS, public Internet, Wifi, cable, DSL, etc. We need the SD-WAN hub or gateway easy to deploy, intelligent, multitenancy, and vCPE thin, white labeled, and plug and play style. We need the SD-WAN control, routing, security, and monitor functions or fabric centrally orchestrated and responsive and quick to execute. Anyway, differentiate the whole SD-WAN solution the best we can.

A: That makes sense. You mention that you want to add more values to the SD-WAN offer. Any success?

V: Sure, for example, we tailor the SD-WAN solutions as Cloud connections, Branch office optimization, or the Overall corporate network re-engineering. Next step, we plan to roll out SD-WAN for IoT and SD-WAN with machine-learning capabilities and big data analytics. The goal is to seamlessly integrate with the next-gen Cloud-powered IT and communication ecosystem.

A: Sounds very promising. I plan to cover more details on service providers' best practice in debuting SD-WAN solution in my new book.

V: Good luck with the new book publishing. Please let us know any time we can be of further assistance.

SD-WAN Brings Strategic New Offers

> Service providers can use a SD-WAN product as a more-flexible, cost-effective alternative to MPLS service, or reach out to new customer segments, such as small or mid-size businesses.

A CSP simply can't survive in today's digital transformation without debuting SD-WAN. Based on their experience and market, CSPs can use the SD-WAN platform, bring value, and create new potential revenue streams as illustrated in Figure 3.1. Compared to traditional WAN, SD-WAN offers more robust and fine-tuned network capabilities and features.

Internally, SD-WAN would accelerate the service provider's transition to Cloud-based SDN/NFV services such as automating key

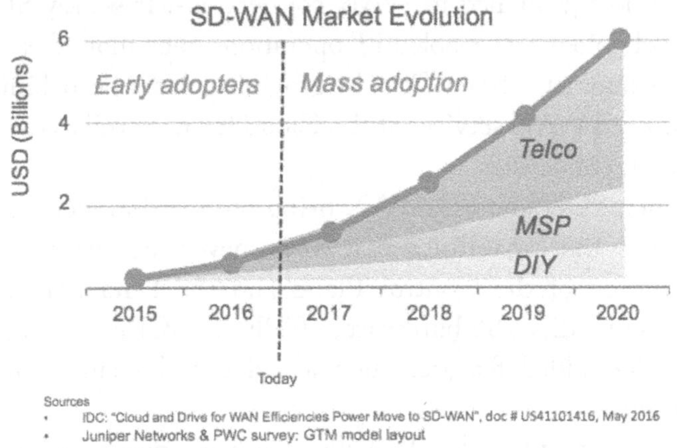

Figure 3.1 Service providers (Telco and MSP) leading the SD-WAN trend.

processes of networking. The future Cloud-based WAN will both speed up and simplify the process of configuring, adding, removing, and managing network services based on business demands and market competitions.

Externally, service providers can use SD-WAN product as a more-flexible, cost-effective alternative to MPLS service, or reach out to new customer segments, such as small or mid-size businesses. For those heavily Cloud-oriented businesses, SD-WAN can bridge interconnects between Cloud providers and enterprises and make a great business expansion solution by quickly serving customers not physically reachable by the service provider's MPLS network. From the invoice accounting perspective, SD-WAN's targeted Class of Services (CoS) from application-based metrics gives the customers a better sense of which applications are using the network and the bandwidth usage associated.

We will elaborate on these key subjects in the following sections.

Revamping Network Operations, Costs, and Services

> SD-WAN is a milestone separating the legacy and next-generation networking and thus possesses strategic implications to service providers' business models and environment.

As discussed in Chapter 1, SD-WAN is a specific implementation of SDN technology applied to WAN connections. If we say SDN as a pivotal technology has enabled IT operations to be more flexible, efficient, and automatic, SD-WAN, by providing similar capabilities, has revolutionized WAN services at the Cloud front as well as the edge of branch and remote sites.

Together, SDN and SD-WAN bring on board modern networking changes and capabilities that we've never seen before, such as the separation of the Control Plane and the Data Plane, operation on commodity x86 hardware, vCPEs or uCPEs in large scale, NFV's value-added features such as advanced security or WAN acceleration.

To service providers, SD-WAN not only is a new solution to offer to the market, but also leads towards the next-generation Cloud networking platform for near future. SD-WAN is a milestone separating the legacy and next-generation networking and thus possesses strategic implications to service providers' business model and environment with revolutionary changes, as highlighted in the following sections.

Service Operation Revolution

Deploying an SD-WAN framework means more intelligence and logic in software rather than in hardware for service providers. The software defined deployment and management advantages are tremendous. Now it's like the network is commanded by a central brain, distributing networking intelligence among the branch device, the service provider edge, and the Cloud as it's appropriate for the deployment and use case.

Software control on an abstraction policy layer is simply increasing flexibility and automation, because it is faster to reprogram devices than it is to procure them and install them one at a time, and also allows service providers to effectively set up and manage all branch office IP Layer WAN connections for the enterprise.

For instance, those previously out of control and "dummy" broadband Internet links, now due to the SD-WAN overlay implementation, can be enhanced in reliability, security, and scalability, which allows providers to route a greater percentage of their network traffic through lower-cost WAN channels.

Cost Saving Revolution

Public Internet overlay and vCPE are two killer cost saving sources for SD-WAN. Internet connections can cost up to 50% less than MPLS links, and vCPEs with zero-touch deployment and management allows service providers to simplify delivery of WAN services to branch offices with little traditional barriers from the hardware deployment side. All this helps to reduce the TCO of WAN services.

Flexibility and fast revenue streams are two other advantages, because service providers can more quickly deploy and provision branch offices, they can start getting revenue faster. Because they can utilize multiple types of WAN links across the enterprise WAN, they can offer more flexibility.

Finally, this central orchestration and control capability from SD-WAN helps to increase the service providers' revenues by handling peak or burst network traffic; bundling higher value-add services to increase customer retention; and providing analysis and enterprise's network traffic status for customer side better management and visibility of the services.

Performance and Service Value Revolution

We've covered the intelligent capabilities of SD-WAN in many previous sections, and that smartness translates into better network performance and customer values to the end users. At the same time, service providers themselves can more easily monitor WAN traffic and lower their troubleshooting and ongoing network management costs.

With no question, direct access to Cloud application and managed services make service value bright spots for SD-WAN. By taking the complexity of private networking out of the equation, the SD-WAN simplifies service delivery channels over public Internet. If some customers might have difficultly managing all of the equipment and setup necessary for an SD-WAN, service providers can also come in and offer managed SD-WAN solutions.

Market Expansion and New Revenue Revolution

SD-WAN can help service providers increase profitability while accommodating WAN market trends. On Day One, SD-WAN won't be an MPLS level revenue machine for the service providers yet due to the cost saving propositions it comes up with to the market. But it will help keeping a service provider in the game, that is, in order to compete and win, service providers need a sound alternative to MPLS or public Internet, a flexible hybrid network solution at lower total cost of ownership as SD-WAN makes a good fit. On an ongoing basis, as the SD-WAN platform grows and enriches its offers, the revenue flow will become bigger consequently.

As already mentioned earlier, service providers don't have to position SD-WAN as an MPLS replacement for existing sites. Rather, they can use SD-WAN's cost-effectiveness as a spear head for new market expansion. Basically, they can capture new customer segments such as SMBs and enterprises in geographical areas where MPLS links are not feasible or available to serve.

Embedding Smart SD-WAN Niches

> WAN is fundamentally about data traffic routing and SD-WAN enhances its routing capabilities with high intelligence and smart control.

Smart SD-WAN makes a disruptive difference with traditional WAN technologies. Being smart and intelligent delivers WAN interconnection through application-level aware path selection, traffic acceleration, and Cloud-based visualized operations and maintenance. Ultimately, it triggers the evolution towards a fully automatic Cloud network for the future.

To better understand SD-WAN's advanced routing capabilities, first we need to get familiar with several approaches a business or service provider can take with WAN network routing.

First, destination or network-based routing: the destination address of a packet gets a route lookup and decides how to route traffic from one point to another. This is the basic approach to WAN routing, and it's how routing has worked since the beginning. It's also how the Internet and most legacy WANs work today.

The problem with destination routing is that it doesn't differentiate WAN applications. All forms of traffic travel from a source to a destination, all taking the same path. Thus it's impossible for an administrator or engineer to change the routing behavior for specific application traffic.

Second, policy-based routing, which makes it possible for a network engineer to determine the WAN routing behavior of certain types of traffic, namely providing Quality of Service (QoS) to differentiated traffic. The so-called policy is defined based on an Access Control List (ACL), which may cover such packet factors as source/destination address and port, protocol, differentiated service code point, and the packet size and classification.

Each incoming packet is matched against the ACL, which allows the network engineer to base the routing decision on more criteria than simply the destination point. This method itself can be applied throughout the network as a whole to route marked traffic along a pre-specified path.

Third, application aware routing, which gets even more granular with specific WAN applications through deep packet inspection (DPI). By figuring out what the application is, the network administrator can give it "special treatment," such as a high priority application of the best possible route or dropping the packets for an application the company has no need for.

Over a legacy network, nevertheless, it's difficult and costly to implement application aware routing in CPE or WAN-edge in large scale; therefore, such application aware routing is typically limited to security appliances.

A granular route lookup also impacts routing and forwarding performance. Excepting destination-based routing, other methods tend to become complicated and busy very quickly for a traditional network. For that reason, they're used sparingly, despite the obvious benefits from like application aware routing.

SD-WAN starts to enable policy or application aware routing, because its software based central controller specifies how all traffic is routed in milliseconds. The controller has the ability to orchestrate the paths between the WAN-edge routers, based on the policy.

SDN enables a network engineer to define a network-wide policy, rather than just a device- or node-level policy. When a business' network requirements change and evolve, the policy is changed in one single place for all. Not only does this reduce the amount of time spent on configuration, but it lowers the likelihood of errors as well.

The result is that the most important applications—truly those with highest priority for a business, such as UC, ERP, collaboration applications, or industry and business-specific applications like telemedicine in healthcare—can rightfully be allowed the highest-quality routes to assure business or customer values. On the other hand, less-important and lower-priority applications can be assigned to the lower-quality paths, or they can be dropped entirely if necessary (Figure 3.2).

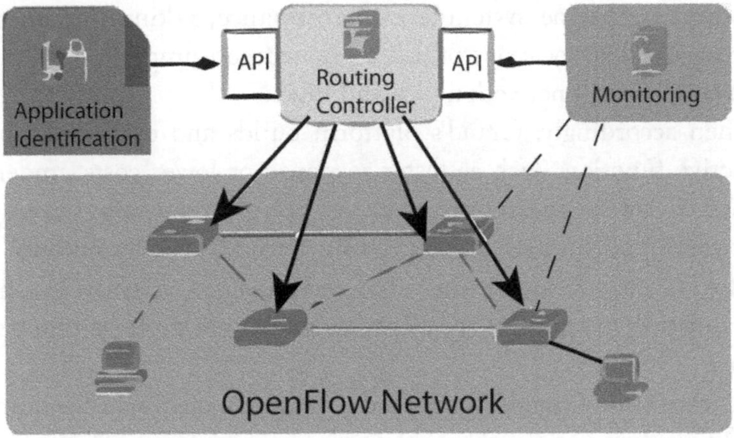

Figure 3.2 Application aware routing network.

A Use Case: Artificial Intelligence for Optimizing Network Paths

Grand Networks, Ltd. is a US Southeast based telecom carrier. In recent years, it has aggressively upgraded its network capabilities to lower the TCO, and better serve new applications and market needs. It has adopted SDN/NFV, AI/machine learning, and SD-WAN as the top three new technologies for service upgrading.

From the traffic routing management perspective, SD-WAN brings new capabilities for Grand Networks to better control and optimize the flow of data traffic with centralized monitoring, SDN controller directs automated operations and distribution of traffic across the system to avoid local choke points, reconfiguring the network to reduce the hops in data flows.

Machine learning, genetic algorithms, and other AI techniques help pinpoint and diagnose the sources of inefficiency like if a route reconfiguration or optimization fails, and come up with possible remedies like quickly constructing private networks on top of existing nodes so as to gain better network control.

In early 2017, Grand Networks signed a managed SD-WAN contract with a large online content provider, with the goal of reshuffling the client's existing network and improving the performance for best savings and performance.

During the process, AL and machine-learning enables Grand to analyze and optimize the client's IP and optical networking holistically rather than as separate layers. First thing first Grand's AI techniques examine system-level performance, taking into account routing options, locations of assets, power consumption, and more, for a collection of network nodes and links.

Then accordingly, Grand's platform builds and optimizes for an objective function, such as faster response or lower costs, under an identified set of constraints, such as policy and energy costs and uncovers opportunities for improving network configurations. The platform's genetic algorithm-based technology can scale its objective function to optimize the client's network with a large number of nodes.

As the result, Grand has realized a reduction of 25% in the number of IP ports between the client's data centers, which not only decreased the costs of moving traffic but also accelerates it over now reduced number of hops in traffic routing.

Launching Managed SD-WAN Services

> The managed SD-WAN solution works out better for national and global deployment and frees the clients from the complexities of day-to-day management of the network and applications so they can focus on moving their business forward.

As described in Chapter 2 from the enterprise user perspective, SD-WAN deployment can come in three flavors: Do it Yourself (DIY), managed services as illustrated in Figure 3.3, and a hybrid model. The DIY model can fit into local and sometimes regional

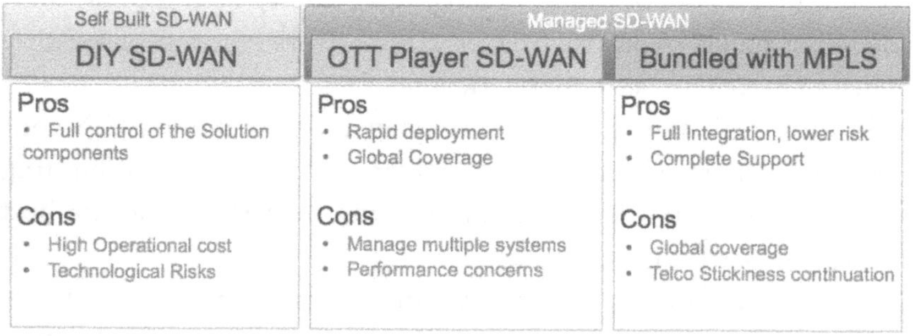
Self Built SD-WAN
Managed SD-WAN
DIY SD-WAN
OTT Player SD-WAN
Bundled with MPLS
Pros
Full control of the Solution components
Cons
High Operational cost
Technological Risks
Pros
Rapid deployment
Global Coverage
Cons
Manage multiple systems
Performance concerns
Pros
Full Integration, lower risk
Complete Support
Cons
Global coverage
Telco Stickiness continuation

Figure 3.3 Managed vs. DIY SD-WAN solutions.

deployment OK when with limited sites and available work resources. The managed SD-WAN solution, on the other hand, works out better for national and global deployment and frees the clients from the complexities of day-to-day management of the network and applications so they can focus on moving their business forward.

WAN management is no doubt a complex process and requires expertise for network managers to run and operate a global WAN. For instance, while an SD-WAN can simplify hybrid WAN setup and initialization, it involves deployment and management of various types of network services that have to support a variety of WAN applications—voice, video, and data—distributed in different IT environments such as on-premise data center, private Cloud, and public Cloud across geographic locations.

This is when the DIY model gets daunting and a managed SD-WAN service will shine. From service convergence perspective, the service provider will bring on expertise and technology to integrate disparate operations and management systems across various access, transport, and network solution providers, presenting a unified view for enterprise network teams.

If the SD-WAN deploys across large geographic areas, the service provider will help to realize the speed of deployment and get the service up and running quickly with good quality control.

Service providers now typically offer free trials to provide businesses the option to evaluate and deploy an SD-WAN in phases. As managed SD-WAN becoming mature into the Cloud network ecosystem, it would help lift many SMB level companies quickly into the Cloud era.

A Use Case of Managed SD-WAN

Tyro Networks, Inc. is an MSP in the US west coast and in early 2017 they rolled out managed SD-WAN services to the market, as increased numbers of branch offices and remote users are driving enterprises to find more efficient and lower-cost methods for WAN connections. Plus, increased use of Cloud services and applications by enterprises calls for more secure and reliable network connectivity.

Tyro is targeting their managed SD-WAN to address these trends head-on, especially for SMBs who don't have in-house expertise to handle the network upgrade and changes. Basically, once a client signs on with SD-WAN, Tyro will deliver and support the edge CPE devices, procure and manage access links from multiple providers, upgrade the technology as it evolves, and manage all day-to-day network aspects of the SD-WAN solution.

Tyro's Managed SD-WAN offers application aware routing that measures and monitors performance of multiple services in the hybrid network with more granular control of where and under what circumstances an application transaction uses a specific service. This allows the enterprise clients to make better use of their overall network because the past dormant capacity in fail-over networks is now included into an active/active configuration.

Tyro's managed solution also allows organizations to offload Internet-bound traffic, which means private WAN services remain available for real-time and mission-critical applications. This added flexibility helps improves traffic flow and alleviates pressure on the corporate network.

Finally, with traditional private WAN services, security is normally implemented fragmentally. Now Tyro's Managed SD-WAN overlays and standardizes a single security policy, often in the form of virtual private network (VPN) tunnels across the entire infrastructure.

Some Insight on SD-WAN's Erosion of MPLS

> $2 Billion revenue gain for SD-WAN might indicate potentially $10–16 billion MPLS revenue erosion for major telcos, which becomes quite a serious wake-up alarm.

Service providers face a changing landscape when it comes to market trends affecting WANs. New competitive options like SD-WAN are cutting into their MPLS revenues; this price erosion is already beginning to appear in negative growth rates for MPLS VPN in Europe in 2017, with North America following suit in 2018 and 2019, and APAC markets next in the queue.

Over the next 5 years to 2023, it's predicted the global MPLS revenue grows only at CAGR 4.1%,* while SD-WAN will enjoy a robust 69.6% CAGR.†

If we say 2017 still sees SD-WAN launches on trial and warm-up basis from numerous service providers, then 2018–2019 will mark the real game kickoff for SD-WAN to take on MPLS in the competitive WAN marketplace. In many cases for the enterprise clients today, SD-WAN has disruptive advantages over MPLS in terms of cost, provisioning, agility, speed, direct connections to Cloud, service redundancy, and management transparency.

Some service providers, such as cable operators Comcast and Charter, will debut their SD-WAN with no legacy MPLS service in the background; while major telcos like AT&T, Verizon, and CenturyLink would have to consider the "cannibalization effect" to their existing MPLS revenues as they roll out their own SD-WAN solutions as well as facing competitions from the cable operators and other SD-WAN players.

Thus these are the two critical questions concerned the major telcos need to address in next two or three years: First, to what extent might SD-WAN take market shares away from MPLS? Second, how will the telcos best maneuver the headwinds of SD-WAN competitions and keep the WAN business healthy?

Based on various forecast sources to date,‡ in 2018 the global MPLS revenue may reach $42.53 billion, and SD-WAN revenue would hit $2 billion. The assumption is most of the $2 billion for SD-WAN would be from the migration of existing MPLS services although at the first sight, this impact seems to be not that significant.

But we need to keep one key caveat in mind: An SD-WAN site service can go 5 to 8 times cheaper than the MPLS counterpart, depending on the particular site circuit status, access configuration, and CoS. This means when a client migrates their WAN service from MPLS to SD-WAN, the MPLS service provider will either lose the account to other vendors or erode the current revenue to a much lower level despite of the rescued client's loyalty.

---

* Research and Markets, MPLS Market Forecast September 21, 2016.
† IDC SD-WAN Market Forecast July 27, 2017.
‡ Grand View Research Global IP VPN MPLS Market April, 2015.

Therefore, $2 billion revenue gain for SD-WAN in 2018 might indicate potentially $10–16 billion MPLS revenue erosion for major telcos, which becomes quite a serious wake-up alarm.

What are the best strategies to handle such looming MPLS revenue cannibalization? There seems to be not a short and simple answer to this challenging situation. The telcos have to do more homework and dive into details on the SD-WAN deployment and competitions in their service territories, and also the impact on different customer use cases, before they can decide on what to do next.

So this new game of SD-WAN vs. MPLS can go in three scenarios. The first scenario would be using pure public Internet (most likely with redundancy from two different ISPs), which means the client would totally unplug the existing MPLS service and switch to high speed SD-WAN with intelligent routing and security package over the public Internet backbone.

In the second scenario, the client may subscribe to SD-WAN over the public Internet but still keep their MPLS service. Via such a hybrid solution hopefully with dynamic load balancing and failover, the client may route non-mission-critical traffic like software usages, email, and storage file transfers over SD-WAN, while still handle mission-critical applications like voice and real-time video over MPLS.

As the result, the client may downsize their MPLS bandwidth for cost saving purpose. For instance, if the site used to take 10 mbps MPLS service, now the client may reduce it to 5 mbps for handling the mission-critical traffic only.

The third scenario is worth more attention over the global network as we elaborate on this subject in the next section. Some service providers may offer to put SD-WAN traffic over their own private Layer 2 backbone, or a hybrid setup with a public Internet access. In this way, their client while leaving an MPLS service provider may still enjoy the CoS and security guaranteed for WAN communications, especially for mission-critical traffic.

While all the three scenarios above could hurt the existing MPLS services, still major telcos should strive for the second scenario, so as to at least prevent the immediate accounts churn and keep the chance alive to make up for the MPLS revenue erosion through developing new value-added services.

From the customer use case perspective, we also see three major models, considering the end user's traffic and application types as well as geographic service coverage.

The first model is for metro and regional level, due to the enhanced Internet quality from dense fiber optic network deployed in recent years, a qualified SD-WAN solution, once tested well, should be capable to replace existing MPLS services, regardless of the traffic and application type being mission-critical or non-critical.

If the WAN service scale is on the national level, the reliability of fiber based and meshed public Internet backbone has also been upgraded significantly. On the safe side, however, adequate tests on the to be frequently used routes should be done first before deciding to adopt pure SD-WAN over the public Internet or use an SD-WAN and MPLS hybrid.

On the international level (discussed in more details in the next section), the common rule of thumb is the public Internet backbone across the North America, Western Europe, and most of Asia Pacific region should be reliable and scalable enough for enterprise applications. But overall, MPLS still has lower levels of packet loss, latency, and jitter than SD-WAN for international long-haul transport.

A multinational enterprise client therefore may want a hybrid MPLS and SD-WAN to handle mission-critical, on-premise, real-time traffic, and those Cloud-based, non-real-time applications, respectively.

It then becomes obvious that those multinational large enterprises are the targets for major telcos to safeguard the existing MPLS revenues. This is not saying the telcos should delay rolling out their own SD-WAN services. The SD-WAN trend is unstoppable and one can only go with the flow or lose to competitions.

To better serve the multinational enterprise segment, the telcos may set up goals of using SD-WAN to augment the existing MPLS services and reinforce the customer loyalty. For example, the hybrid MPLS and SD-WAN service can be applied to more branch and remote sites (including IoT applications), and Cloud applications for the enterprise clients.

What's Special in Global Long-Haul SD-WAN Solution?

> As a solution to the underlay network bottleneck causing global application delivery issues via SD-WAN, a global private network that provides the flexibility of the public Internet and the reliability of MPLS is in need.

As mentioned in the section above, people often see SD-WAN as an innovative solution riding over the public Internet, bidding farewell to the private network solutions like MPLS traverses on. In reality this is not always the case. In April 2018, an US California HQed SD-WAN service provider Aryaka Networks announced that it will partner with China Mobile International (CMI) to deliver a global SD-WAN service, targeting multinational businesses with locations in China as well as Chinese companies that have a global presence. This reminds us of a different approach SD-WAN can take on its services.

In the long list of SD-WAN service providers, Aryaka differentiates itself with it being able to deliver SD-WAN and network optimization via its own "global private network," which to date serves over 7,000 sites in 63 countries.

As we know, one of the killer features of SD-WAN is to ride on an overlay of the public Internet, which can save tons of cost bypassing the traditional WAN technologies like private MPLS service, and also offer a robust performance for direct Cloud access and applications.

However, while the overlay-based SD-WAN may be an answer for US local and regional deployments, it is hardly the answer for global WAN requests, with the reason being the underlay still has to leverage the public Internet or a hybrid scenario that includes both the public Internet and MPLS links for specific applications.

Here is the problem: From the global standpoint, the performance and availability of public Internet to date vary drastically from country to country, and region to region and its quality, especially in terms of network latency and packet loss, can easily run out of control.

For instance, from San Jose to Shanghai, the latency measurement for public Internet is 3.97 seconds, while private network only

0.306 s. In addition, packet loss often ranges from 10%–15% over the Internet between branch offices located in San Jose and China, which results in data having to be sent through the network over and over again.

This would make a huge difference for enterprise users who need to transfer some large in size, time sensitive, Cloud-based, and mission-critical workloads like SAP Business ByDesign ERP or Salesforce.com. As a rule of thumb, around 0.3 second of network latency is technically acceptable to most of business digital applications nowadays, while anything over 2% packet loss over a period of time is a strong indicator of problems.

In another instance of testing, using public Internet connectivity, application response time transferring file between Dubai and Dallas was between 0.75 and 2 seconds, and a different route testing for the same locations has resulted in between 0.127 and 4 seconds. Such performance variation and inconsistency for the network underlay apparently can't serve the business class SD-WAN successfully.

Aryaka claims that in order to solve this underlay network bottleneck causing global application delivery issues via the public Internet, they have built up, via leasing, transit, colocation, etc., a global private network for its SD-WAN that provides the flexibility of the public Internet and the reliability of MPLS. The private network not only provides secure access to data and applications from the corporate data center, but also to any Cloud and SaaS environment.

For the local access leg, Aryaka's model seemingly is to partner with different regional and local ISPs. In the China Mobile International case, for example, CMI will sell SD-WAN to Chinese enterprises and also local circuits for a complete solution. One popular local solution is using dual Internet services. For much less money than MPLS, end user can support each location with at least two Internet pipes like 50 mbps or 100 mbps or more at their choice running to different POPs. Via such "dual Internet local access" customer enjoys more redundancy, better bandwidth, and full support.

Something that we haven't heard Aryaka touting much is the overall cost associated with its SD-WAN service. We may assume it would cost somewhere between the overlay network-based SD-WAN and private MPLS. After all, business customer nowadays would be willing to pay some premium for global SD-WAN services that run over private backbone with dual Internet local access but still being cheaper than using a traditional MPLS solution.

Another example is Google. For more than 10 years, Google has been building its own private network infrastructure to support new, effectively real-time services that span the globe. About 3 years ago, Google launched Espresso—the fourth part of its SDN strategy, extending its SDN approach to the peering edge of the network—where it allows Google to balance traffic based on actual performance data and to react in real-time to failures and congestion, as well as to separate the logic and control of traffic management from the individual router boxes.

All in all, next-generation WAN solutions would boil down to some tradeoffs amid network performance, business applications, and service costs associated. Aryaka's approach seems to be positioning itself well and providing a sound SD-WAN solution in the global scale, and Google via SDN can exercise more control of the network flow and security. It is expected that the use of private networks will be the future for the global long-haul SD-WAN solutions.

SD-WAN Isn't Just Another WAN

According to the market status of first half of 2018, while SD-WAN adoption by enterprises of all sizes and verticals is accelerating, there are some barriers along the road as well. When being introduced on SD-WAN, at the strategic level, enterprises may have these three typical concerns or objections. First, our MPLS services are working fine and SD-WAN sounds like just another WAN option over the broadband Internet. We don't have a big zeal for it.

Second, we can see from your presentation and demo that SD-WAN is a fantastic technology and cost-saving. But it might add up complexity in our network management if we take on the MPLS and SD-WAN hybrid approach. Also, our organizational structure and staff training are not ready yet for SD-WAN and we still face some learning curves.

Third, SD-WAN is good but we would wait for a while and see, because we are in a strategic juncture of putting all the puzzles together for the Digital Age, like what to do with Cloud, security, mobility, big data, IoT, AI, etc. We hesitate to just single SD-WAN adoption out at this point of time.

All interesting comments but they do come with misunderstanding or wrong perception on SD-WAN. By all means, enterprises should think big on SD-WAN today, or you may lose big tomorrow. We can think big on SD-WAM from the following three perspectives.

First, SD-WAN is the main bloodline or central glue of the next-generation IT ecosystem, which will enable the so-called digital transformation (DX) for the future enterprise world. While nearly all the businesses today want to use Cloud and mobility, add up security, and take advantage of big data, it's SD-WAN which connects all these new utilities and applications together. Or say without SD-WAN, the DX can't happen. Hence, it's not a good strategy to postpone your engagement with SD-WAN.

Second, some may ask: can't legacy services like MPLS or public Internet handle DX for us as well? And they provide good network services to us today. Well, MPLS and public Internet might support some basic digital services, but as things advance (e.g., needs for Cloud direct access), legacy networks would turn out as being ineffective, long lead time, costly, unreliable, unscalable, and insecure.

More importantly, SD-WAN is not just another WAN, like in the past ATM and frame relay replacing private line, and then MPLS and Ethernet taking over ATM and frame relay. SD-WAN goes way beyond a sole network transmission solution and brings about a new digital service platform where you can scale and add on applications and solutions (e.g., enhanced firewall package and machine learning functions), and segment network operation as well as application performance.

Why can SD-WAN make a digital service platform while MPLS remains only a network transport solution? The key difference comes from that SD-WAN is powered by SDN and NFV that create a central and unified network controlling fabric and apply complex network functions virtually in a widely distributed manner. On the contrary, MPLS is mostly hardware centric network with fragmented control points that are difficult to monitor, upgrade, and orchestrate.

This also leads to our third angle on SD-WAN: being software defined and system virtualized makes an intelligent next-generation network possible, in contrast to the dumb or semi-dumb legacy networks we may still use today. An intelligent network includes two major features. The first is automation vs. a lot of work like network upgrade, new provisioning, trouble shooting, policy change, and implementation that used to be handled and completed manually. Automation means flexibility, simplicity, and high efficiency.

The second feature is by using Cloud-based AI and machine learning functions, the next-generation network can process big data collected real time and quickly identify problem, fraud and security breach patterns, and then come up with the right responses and solutions, like securely routing and prioritizing mission critical applications. Together with edge computing and modular data centers, the intelligent network can serve well the enterprises either connecting people or things toward the Digital Age.

Once we get out of the box perceiving SD-WAN only as another WAN, it will open the holistic new view with SD-WAN as the key entry platform and enabler for DX. If realizing the future IT ecosystem will mostly be about SDx, e.g., SD-WAN, SD-DC, SD-Storage, SD-IoT, etc., then it makes great sense for enterprises to start off this exciting journey by adopting SD-WAN solutions now.

Effective Go-to-Market Approaches for SD-WAN

> It takes an effective campaign of positioning, bundling, target marketing, and up-selling for SD-WAN to win the market.

By the end of 2018, SD-WAN is expected to be adopted by 60% of enterprises as a critical component of remote branch connectivity according to IDC predictions.* Enterprises are looking to achieve massive cost savings by moving traffic from MPLS to the Internet, but not only that, they are also interested in providing better support for high-bandwidth applications, simplifying traffic management, and accelerating the deployment of new branch locations.

With enterprise applications moving to the Cloud, SD-WAN is well positioned to facilitate this transition. In addition to a killer product, SD-WAN also needs an effective Go-to-Market strategy to be successful. For service providers, it's not just a simple matter of new

* IDC FutureScape: Worldwide Telecommunications 2018 Predictions issued on November 29, 2017.

service launch. Rather it takes an effective campaign of positioning, bundling, target marketing, and up-selling for SD-WAN to win the market.

Each vendor should choose its own appropriate Go-to-Market strategy. Large telecom carriers or MSPs are mostly launching SD-WAN as speak more from a deepening the WAN portfolio and providing alternative and value-add solutions perspective to their enterprise market. Hybrid SD-WAN service of MPLS and Internet leads the mainstream in this sector.

A smart way for the cable operators to enter the SD-WAN market while beating the learning curve for WAN service is to start small, like using SD-WAN to securely and stably link small and medium businesses (SMB) to some popular Cloud applications like Office 365, Salesforce.com, etc. Then gradually they can ramp up the WAN network competition against the telcos in full scale.

Meanwhile, some large equipment or infrastructure vendor may start to spot the momentum of SD-WAN and envision a roadmap moving forward for this new solution. As the result, they start to snap on those SD-WAN pure play vendors into their pockets as a key add-up to their strategic product portfolio. For example, in mid and late 2017 Cisco bought Viptela and VMWare acquired VeloCloud, respectively.

Some other medium or Tier-3 and -4 telcos may still feel concerned that SD-WAN doesn't have complete standards uniformity yet and the overhead in having the standards in place is still relatively significant. Meanwhile, they may have incumbent MPLS revenue to protect. So, they may want to wait longer for the technology maturity and trial more for the best selections on the vendors.

A successful SD-WAN Go-To-Market (Figure 3.4) should follow these few principles: First, service providers should investigate the SD-WAN market, establish relevance, and position a product offer in order to optimize the chance of market success.

Second, the SD-WAN products must be easily adopted and bundled for enterprises to consume, as the comparable MPLS is a fully managed single vendor provided offering with a simple purchase process.

Third, service providers need to focus on a few key verticals that may most likely adopt SD-WAN. At this point enterprises from

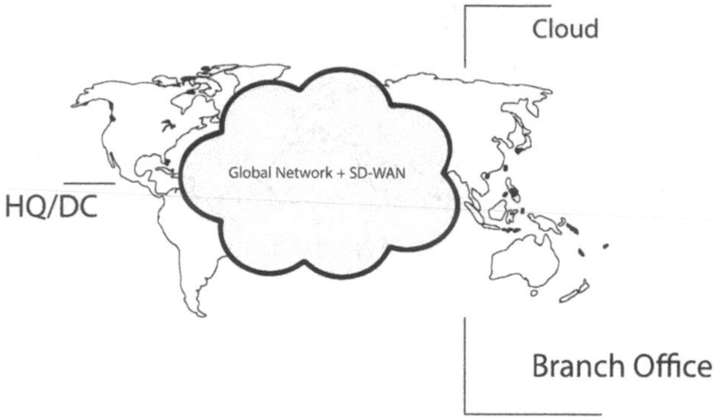

Figure 3.4 SD-WAN Go-to-Market.

retail, finance, and healthcare who are eager to cut their WAN cost and obtain high speeds Cloud direct connections are at the top of user profile for SD-WAN.

Fourth, significant investments need being made in customer education and free trial of the value proposition. SD-WAN may appear to be yet another buzzword within the broader SDN and NFV technologies universe, so there are outstanding misconceptions associated with its relevance and scope that need being demystified.

We will cover these principles in more details in sections that follow.

Service Positioning and Bundling

> The firm's marketing group is instructed to find an optimal way in launching SD-WAN and one viable approach is to do solution bundling.

SD-WAN could very well be a chance for service providers to improve customer experience, increase stickiness, and reduce churn rates. Strategically we see two categories of SD-WAN vendors nowadays: Those who have existing MPLS services like most of the telecom carriers or telcos; and those who don't have legacy MPLS services like the cable operators and pure play startups.

For the first category, those service providers can position SD-WAN as a supplemental solution and enhance their positioning with existing customers; to new sites and territories, the service providers can proactively target new customers, workloads, or regions, and partner with out-of-region providers and quickly set up and provision SD-WAN. Also, we see some SD-WAN vendors bundle higher capacity broadband and value-added services, such as analytics and security for successfully upselling to existing MPLS clients.

The second category of vendors should view SD-WAN as a pure growth opportunity and pursue an accordingly aggressive sales strategy to capture market share from dominant MPLS providers. Tactically these vendors can position the SD-WAN solution and its bundling in the market to address those pain points (as illustrated in Figure 3.5) the clients have with their existing WAN services, convergence, or new service demands with lower cost.

As we already discussed in previous sections, the major pain points from MPLS services including unsatisfactory connectivity to Cloud service and SaaS application; complex and costly branch office infrastructure and long provisioning cycle; on site back up circuit idle but expensive; and hard to make consistent and secure changes to the network, etc.

If the client is currently using conventional public Internet for their business communications, then the pain points may include: lack of

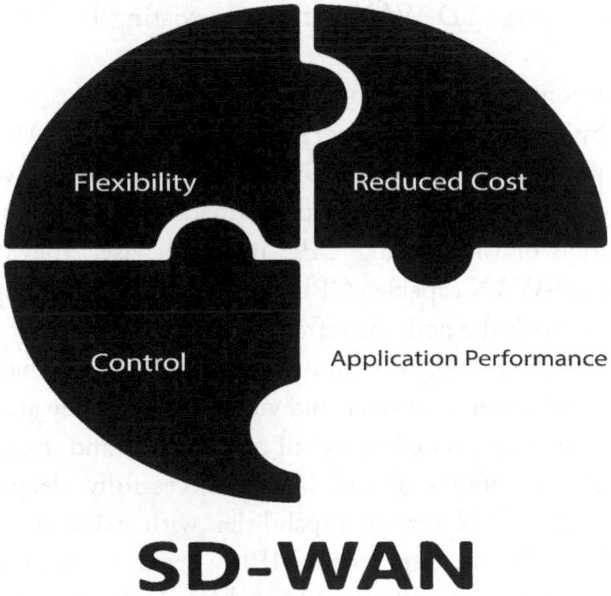

Figure 3.5 Positioning SD-WAN capabilities.

guaranteed predictable performance and SLA for the service; lack of resiliency and high availability in networking; and lack of a centralized orchestration console for managing and modifying application QoS and security policies.

A Use Case of Effective SD-WAN GTM

Speed Communications, Inc. is an incumbent telecom carrier serving the US market nationwide with a large size of MPLS customers and sites. In summer 2017, the executive team of the company made a decision to roll out SD-WAN to the market. But the challenges of potential MPLS revenue erosion was real and SD-WAN service revenues won't easily offset the predicted revenue loss from MPLS.

So, the firm's marketing group is instructed to find an optimal way in launching SD-WAN and one viable approach is to do solution bundling. Instead of separating each WAN solution as like MPLS, SD-WAN, Ethernet, dedicated T1, 4GLTE, satellite, etc., now Speed is bundling all solutions in a portfolio re-branded as "Speed Digital Links." The portfolio can organically piece a holistic WAN solution together for the client based on their traffic types, sites, regions, budget, and operation models and seamlessly integrate and converge SD-WAN with their existing IP VPN offering like MPLS.

Furthermore, this new portfolio takes a more comprehensive approach by integrating additional services with their SD-WAN offering, such as security, WAN optimization, and analytics & visibility.

The Speed SD-WAN task group also made great efforts to address the transition of the existing CPE installed base. They've started deploying SD-WAN capable vCPEs in new locations and update the existing sites with the periodic refresh in next 3 years. The SD-WAN vCPEs add more intelligence into SD-Wan solutions to handle real-time communications like voice and video, because they are remotely controlled and orchestrated across all transport IP and session layers.

With all the efforts above, Speed successfully deepened and enriched their WAN service capabilities with existing customers, having effectively protected their MPLS revenue; meanwhile they aggressively signed on 150 new SD-WAN clients in 6 months and added up new revenue stream.

Market Segmentation and Targeting

Major US telecom carriers (telcos) and MSPs are now all pushing for massive SD-WAN deployment to augment their WAN solutions or even replace the legacy network architecture and functionalities. Figure 3.6 clearly illustrates the trend of SD-WAN adoption.

With all these SD-WAN deployments and launching campaigns underway, the next mission for the service providers will be about how to effectively promote and sell SD-WAN to the marketplace. Whenever a new technology emerges, there will be some early adopters, but carrying on the new service quickly into the mainstream market may become quite a challenge. While SD-WAN offers quite attractive savings, features, and lead-time, some enterprises might remain skeptical on factors like standards and technology maturity, integration with existing architecture, reliability SLA, traffic security, and control power on the network.

In order to speed up the market adoption of SD-WAN, while in the back office the service providers should continue to work closely with equipment vendors to upscale and standardize the new SD-WAN architecture and ecosystem, for the front office, on the other hand, service providers will need to determine the key demand drivers that make SD-WAN relevant for businesses. Market segmentation mistakes and inaccurate sales targeting, on the other hand, can result in poor market penetration, high sales costs, and cannibalization of existing MPLS business.

Mid-Market, Enterprise Timeframe for SD-WAN Implementation

Already deployed	27%
Within six months	44%
Within 12 months	21%
Within 24 months	6%
No plans	2%

Source: IDG Connect, Silver Peak survey of 160 companies

Figure 3.6 SD-WAN adoption rate in the US as of 2017.

The following are the five primary sales & marketing targets for SD-WAN. First, existing heavy but unhappy MPLS users. For those enterprises (e.g., banks, retailers, and manufacturers) with over 30 MPLS regional or national sites currently, especially when those sites are made of many branch offices across large geographic areas, maintaining, troubleshooting, and upgrading this MPLS network can become quite a pain in terms of cost, resources, and time. Thus SD-WAN offers may become an easy sale pitch to these enterprise users. The sound approach is to identify the pain points with the current MPLS service and then offer SD-WAN as a cure, or at least a partial cure like a hybrid solution to replace some of the MPLS connections.

For example, in the US market less than 70% of large companies have offices in 10+ states and more than 50% of employees outside HQ. Typically, businesses with dispersed locations and employees will have a greater interest in SD-WAN, and this 70% client base from the large business sector should be identified, prioritized, and may lead to better conversion rates.

Initial sales efforts should focus on these prospective customers. But the caveat is, as already discussed in previous sectors, sales efforts need to be well targeted as service providers do not want to cannibalize their own MPLS business by inappropriately selling to existing customers who are not suited to migrate to SD-WAN in the near-term.

Second, those enterprises that generate heavy video traffic and on a CDN (content delivery network) platform. Video content includes both regular recreational stream (e.g., from YouTube and online gaming) and business critical purpose like video conferencing, and they take a lot of bandwidth away in network transport. Hence, it is beneficial to distinguish them and keep the business-critical only video traffic over MPLS and allocate and reroute those recreational video traffic to SD-WAN, which can lead to better cost and bandwidth control to the enterprise clients.

Third, the SMB sector. Some misunderstanding is SD-WAN is only suited for large enterprises. As a matter of fact, SD-WAN will fit well to those SMBs who want to link their branch offices and remote working employees via an Intranet or directly to Cloud but cannot afford MPLS or have issues with legacy IP VPN services.

In such scenarios, the service provider should first try to get a better feel about the client's cost sensitivity and average IT budget, and then accordingly design the SD-WAN package that may include both public Internet and 4G LTE wireless connections, because for those customers who feel a wireline Internet connection not available to pursue, then a 4G LTE solution with up to 300 mbps download and 75 mbps upload speed can be the right choice.

Forth, those enterprises that have largely adopted Cloud Infrastructure as a Service (IaaS) and Software as a Service (SaaS). For these Cloud-know-how customers, since they've taken the initial step to virtualize their IT operations and architecture, now it should make a lot of sense for them to virtualize and simplify their network connectivity as well, based on the same Cloud centric technologies towards a new ecosystem.

Currently they may use a private MPLS and public Internet hybrid to handle their Cloud communications, but tomorrow they will be better off to use a new hybrid: Private MPLS for mission-critical data, and SD-WAN for regular data, which is more cost-effective, managed, and secured.

Finally, those IoT and M2M (machine to machine) service providers and users. These clients have been struggling between a private MPLS and public Internet. The former can be too much for IoT and M2M applications, while the latter can be vulnerable and uncertain in reliability and security. So now SD-WAN can come up as the best solution to handle IoT and M2M traffic over the IP network globally.

Besides, service providers should offer more educational and training programs, proof of concept, free trial, use cases and testimonials, etc. to better promote and sell SD-WAN into the market. If we say 2016 was the year of SD-WAN deployment from the service providers' standpoint, 2017 started early SD-WAN adoption from enterprises, then 2018 and beyond will become the years of SD-WAN adoption for the enterprise mainstream, in particular for those enterprises as profiled and targeted above.

Tips of SD-WAN Sale Engagement

> It's successful sales who will eventually champion SD-WAN in the marketplace.

With the right positioning, bundling, targeting, and profiling strategies in place, SD-WAN still requires a knowledgeable and solution-oriented sales force to engage the clients, upsell the solutions, and materialize the revenues. It's successful sales who will eventually champion SD-WAN in the marketplace.

So, when facing a client, how does a salesperson effectively pitch SD-WAN through and get some sales brewing? From consultative technology sales perspective, a salesperson should listen well first and obtain a firm understanding of the client current and future needs, their existing services, pain points, current cost vs. planned budget, etc. before pitching the client on a solution.

Fundamentally a salesperson may come across three types of leads with regard to SD-WAN sales. The first type may have an existing WAN service like MPLS, but know little about SD-WAN yet. They can be conservative in making changes on their incumbent WAN service. The second type have an existing MPLS or dedicated T1 solutions for WAN, and have also heard about the SD-WAN concept. They may be open for new technology and solutions. The third type own existing MPLS and have also done their homework on SD-WAN. They are actively searching for a qualified SD-WAN solution and vendor but can also be picky in making their final selections.

In general, sales efforts should intensify as chances of sales closing increase. SD-WAN sales would not happen like a slam dunk mostly because it's a new technology and most enterprise prospects would take cautions in the front to assess, understand, try out the new solution, and hopefully can embrace it by the end.

Leads Type I–Proof of Concept and Use Case Presentation

For the first type of leads, sales may want to focus on SD-WAN solution introduction and education, with the goal of increasing the client's awareness of the new WAN service and option now on the table. All marketing efforts like workshop, webinars, trade shows, and executive briefings should target general enterprise audience for SD-WAN solution awareness and education.

One effective way is for Sales to present use cases (Figure 3.7 shown as a good reference) to the potential clients. If the clients remain

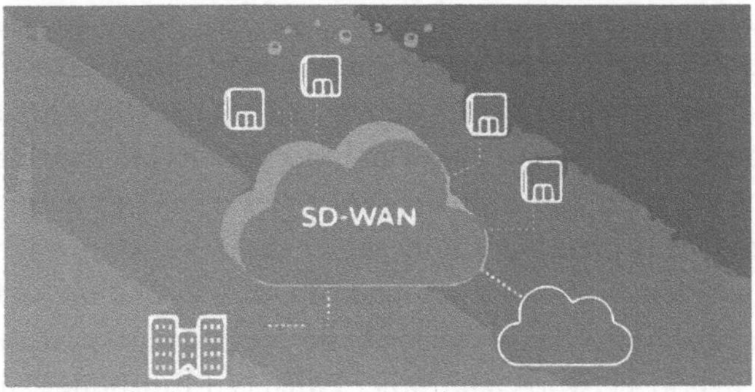

Figure 3.7 SD-WAN use cases.

interested after learning the use cases, then start to go through the SD-WAN solution details.

So far, we've covered plenty of use cases in the book from both concept awareness and key feature applications. In general, SD-WAN sales team should keep at least three typical SD-WAN use cases handy including branch office WAN augmentation, MPLS Replacement or Hybrid WAN, and vCPE applications, because these three types represent the most disruptive changes SD-WAN can bring abroad to the potential enterprise clients.

Leads Type II–Solution Consulting and Planning Assistance

For the second type of leads, the salesperson can focus on the SD-WAN solution the firm he or she represents can offer. May need some consultative work in the front like Business Case and ROI analysis to get the attention of the decision makers for a potential SD-WAN adoption.

Specifically, to enable an SD-WAN sale, the salesperson together with sales engineers may want help the client to do some assessment or planning on applications to determine flow and performance thresholds and routing rules. Also, the sales team can help the client research various options and their associated costs, e.g., ROI, comparing the cost of switching to SD-WAN with building new private network capacity the traditional way.

By doing the above planning work, the sales team from the service provider also gains a better understanding of customer's use cases and networking challenges. When it comes to WAN networking connectivity, no two customers are alike. So, what are the issues customer faces with their current network infrastructure? Do they plan to deploy a hybrid WAN architecture? If the client has a Cloud migration strategy, what services and applications are they looking to invest in? What are the customer's resources or budget restrictions?

After all this prep work done, then the sales team might reach a good position to propose a sound SD-WAN solution and design recommendation to the client for better network performance, cost control, hybrid network, and other enhanced capabilities like data analytics.

Leads Type III–Service Niches and Implementation Offering

For the third type of leads, most likely they are fine with the mainstream SD-WAN solution elements and features offered from the service vendors, but based on their business particular needs and growth, they may want some special bundling into the SD-WAN service such as enhanced security and regulatory compliance, expedited provisioning, or advanced edge intelligence to deal with IoT traffic, etc., as well as a more competitive commercial offering.

If for instance an enterprise wants to take advantage of videoconferencing and collaboration applications, but they don't want to over-provision their network bandwidth, SD-WAN lets them use the bandwidth they need when they need it, and then turn it off. Some other firms may need IT and networking support in mergers and acquisitions, and have to integrate sites more quickly, SD-WAN speeds up the process and can segment secured zones for the M&A activities. Also, many companies today deploy intelligent sensors and other devices, i.e., IoT, SD-WAN will support millions of connections and the data flowing between the networks at a more cost-effective manner.

As a good value addition, the salesperson can also prospect the implementation process to the client.

Some enterprises might be hesitant about conducting a complete overhaul of their WAN, replacing it with a technology that's relatively new to them. Instead they would prefer to conduct free trial first and upgrade in phases, based on their current position in the market and where they expect to be in the future.

From the angle of the client's current telecom model, the sales team can propose what changes will need to be made to successfully integrate SD-WAN. If the client has recently made an investment in WAN infrastructure, they might be interested in a hybrid SD-WAN approach.

Multi-location companies may want assurance their service provider can offer consistent service nationwide. If they plan to open more locations, they'll need a provider with full coverage in their strategic growth areas.

And most importantly, sales team need to walk the client through all reliability and security concerns to ensure they understand their data will be secure and their business will keep running 24/7. Most enterprises will need assurance that an SD-WAN solution will give them heightened network reliability and security, otherwise their SD-WAN decision may get stuck or even held back there. Therefore, sales should know well how to address these two main issues with a game plan so as to get over the barriers and move the sale process forward.

Trend on Sales and Service Automation

> Such sale process automating tool enables sales reps, channels, and agent partners to quickly deliver solution design, multi-carrier circuit quoting, pricing, provisioning, and ultimately increase sales of SA-WAN.

Another new trend, in contrast to the traditionally tedious and time-consuming sourcing and negotiation between client prospects and service providers for a WAN deal, is for service providers to automate the SD-WAN service designing and provisioning process via some software driven Service Portal, so as to shorten the sales process and time to market.

Such software powered service portal can integrate sales leads like from Salesforce.com with the big data mining of telecom infrastructure intelligence to create a core mapping and visualization platform. Via a custom API, sales and sales engineers can access the platform and visualize market data and network assets and gain access to real-time analytics on fiber routes and buildings.

For instance, sales team can use the real-time location intelligence to more effectively design and deliver competitively priced and diversely routed network services. Such sale process automating tool enables sales reps, channels, and agent partners to quickly deliver solution design, multi-carrier circuit quoting, pricing, provisioning, and ultimately increase sales of SA-WAN.

In the latest development, some service providers are even trying to "remove sales people" in the middle and allow potential clients to access such automated service portal to pick and subscribe themselves what they need for SD-WAN. As long as the potential client owns the technical know-how to set up their WAN, they can build their SD-WAN based on proximity, price, time to deploy, and QoS, etc. directly from the automated service portal from the service provider and also become a true part of the next-generation WAN service ecosystem.

In the next 3-5 years, we expect to see a mix of traditional sales and the tools of sales automation. As the network itself becomes more intelligent, software-defined, and open-structured, more direct client and provider interaction via robust APIs and sales automation would take place.

Conclusion

Toward Fully-Fledged Next-Gen Networking

Clearly now we've entered the stage of massive SD-WAN service implementation. We expect to see an exponential growth of SD-WAN in the market in the next 3–5 years. This not only unfolds the WAN service powered by SDN/NFV but also may eventually lead to Cloud-based and AI-powered global WAN networking (Figure C.1).

All this is shaping the innovative trends and services for the enterprise market. For instance, AT&T is poised to achieve SDN network transformation goal to 65% in 2018.* Verizon sees network virtualization as a robust opportunity to cut its costs by $10 billion by 2020.† Juniper is bringing AI bots to Intent-based networks, which basically leverages the capabilities of SDN and marries it to intelligence. Juniper's Bots facilitate automation by making it easier for people to interact with their network.‡

On the SD-WAN launch and adoption fronts, one interesting example is: back in early April 2017, it was reported that: "Comcast, Charter, Altice, other Large Cable MSOs Remain Mum on SD-WAN Plans,"§ but only in a couple of months, Comcast announced they will enter the SD-WAN market, then by late October, Charter joined the SD-WAN debut too. From this example, we can feel the fast pace of SD-WAN entering the market.

Of course, this doesn't mean we encourage any rush to SD-WAN offer or market. Due diligence such as planning, forecast, positioning, as this book attempts to cover and elaborate, needs to be in place first so that an enterprise or service provider can take the biggest advantage of SD-WAM services.

Using the cable operators as an example again, while they may not have a legacy MPLS network to worry about as the telecom carriers

* RCRWireless News, July 2, 2018.

† RCRWireless News, November 10, 2017.

‡ Networkworld.com, December 20, 2017.

§ FierceTelecom.com, April 13, 2017.

Figure C.1 A global Cloud WAN.

do, they are not very experienced with WAN network solutions yet, especially in terms of managed services. Their teams need to build up expertise in jobs including access links aggregation, SD-WAN solution deployment and management, and multiple WAN services and partners management on the network.

For enterprise end users, the adoption of SD-WAN is also a value evolving process. Whereas SD-WAN was initially thought of an overlay that abstracts the transport network and provides direct and cost-effective links to the Cloud for branches, it is evolving to be more about a robust digital platform for application-driven policy routing, analytics, and enhanced security.

As for the industry and solution standard uniformity, although SD-WAN tends to be built with open source hardware and software, it doesn't automatically make SD-WAN itself open. Some industry standard and protocols that allow multivendor SD-WAN integration and interoperability are still due.

Ultimately, SD-WAN should bring about an open and cooperative service platform, implement VNFs, and support rapid and automatic provisioning. The SD-WAN controller must be able to quickly interconnect with operations and business support systems (OSS/BSS) and third-party application systems like the public Clouds.

A comprehensive Industry survey* found significant difference between pre and post SD-WAN adoption for enterprises. The key drivers for those who planned to adopt SD-WAN were, in order of

* PricewaterhouseCoopers survey in collaboration with Juniper conducted in November 2016.

priority: 1. cost of WAN service; 2. migration to Cloud; 3. increased flexibility; 4. ease of use; 5. more automation.

However, once adopted, SD-WAN has changing priorities for enterprises: 1. increased flexibility; 2. more automation; 3. cost of WAN service; 4. ease of use; 5. migration to Cloud.

This survey shows the trend as driving the enterprise IT and network operation and service towards a Cloud and AI-powered digital ecosystem in the near future. It's a fast-moving bullet train. Don't miss it, or you may fall behind in this advanced Digital Age.

Glossary of Networking and SD-WAN Solutions

4G LTE (Long-Term Evolution): a wireless data communication standard that uses digital signal processing (DSP) techniques to increase the speed and capacity of wireless data networks. LTE must bc used on a separate radio spectrum because it is incompatible with 2G and 3G networks.

Access control list (ACL): a list of access control entries (ACEs). Each ACE in an ACL identifies a trustee and specifies the access rights allowed, denied, or audited for that trustee.

Advanced encryption standard (AES): a symmetric block cipher chosen by the U.S. government to protect classified information and is implemented in software and hardware throughout the world to *encrypt* sensitive data.

Application aware routing (AAR): in the context of SD-WAN, AAR is the intelligent forwarding of application traffic across the enterprise WAN ensuring that pre-defined, per-application performance metrics, or service level agreements (SLA), are persistently met at the lowest achievable costs.

Application program interface (API): code that allows two software programs to communicate with each other. The ***API*** defines the correct way for a developer to write a program that requests services from an operating system (OS) or other application.

Artificial intelligence (AI, also machine intelligence, MI): intelligence displayed by machines, in contrast with the natural intelligence (NI) displayed by humans and other animals. In computer science, AI research is defined as the study of "intelligent agents": any device that perceives its environment and takes actions that maximize its chance of success at some goal.

Asynchronous transfer mode (ATM): a switching technique used by telecommunication networks that uses asynchronous time-division multiplexing to encode data into small, fixed-sized cells. It is different from Ethernet or Internet, which use variable packet sizes for data or frames. ATM is the core protocol used over the synchronous optical network (SONET) backbone of the integrated digital services network (ISDN).

Border gateway protocol (BGP): used for end-to-end routing on WAN networks. It exchanges routing information between independent systems on the Internet. When a circuit fails, BGP reroutes traffic to a secondary route, after a short delay, to prevent a complete WAN failure. Because BGP lacks application-specific intelligence, PfR may be a better alternative.

Botnet threats: a collection of Internet-connected devices, which may include PCs, servers, mobile devices, and Internet of Things devices that are infected and controlled by a common type of malware. Users are often unaware of a *botnet* infecting their system.

Bring Your Own Device (BYOD): refers to the trend of employees bringing their personal mobile devices to work and connecting them to enterprise networks. This post discusses challenges, associated with co-mingling personal and corporate information, and strategies for addressing them.

Bursting: enables network to accommodate spikes in bandwidth demand. A handful of carriers support bursting on their IP-VPN networks. Bursting can be very cost-effective because it lets customers commit to the least amount of bandwidth they need for continued use and pay for only what they use in excess of that amount.

Class of Service (CoS): enables organizations to assign some types of traffic classification priority over others. By doing so, they can get better performance out of the network without spending money on unnecessary bandwidth. There are several CoS treatments for MPLS networks.

Command-line interface (CLI): a traditional means of interacting with a computer program where the user (or client) issues commands to the program in the form of successive lines of text.

Communications services provider (CSP): Encompasses a broad range of service providers including telecom service providers, MSOs, network service providers, and wireless service providers.

Content delivery network or content distribution network (CDN): a large distributed system of servers deployed in multiple data centers across the Internet that provide end-users with high availability and high performance.

Control plane: the part of a network that carries signaling traffic and is responsible for routing. Control packets originate from or are destined for a router.

Data deduplication: the process of identifying redundant data segments and storing only one instance of information. Data deduplication dramatically reduces storage space and allows enterprises to protect more data over time.

Data plane: (sometimes known as the user plane, forwarding plane, carrier plane, or bearer plane) the part of a network that carries user traffic. The data plane, the control plane and the management plane are the three basic components of a telecommunications architecture.

Deep packet inspection (DPI): (also called complete packet inspection and information extraction or IX) a form of computer network packet filtering that examines the data part (and possibly also the header) of a packet as it passes an inspection point, searching for protocol non-compliance, viruses, spam, intrusions.

Denial of Service (DoS) attack: attempt to make a network resource unavailable to its users that creates a bottleneck on and greatly reduces network speeds for its duration. With a direct connection to the Internet, IP VPN over Internet is vulnerable to DoS attacks.

Destination-based routing: the typical, most common type of routing. For this, each message that we send contains the address of the destination and the forwarding decision process makes its forwarding decision solemnly based on this address (and independent of the original sender).

Digital transformation: the profound transformation of business and organizational activities, processes, competencies, and models to fully leverage the changes and opportunities of a mix of digital technologies and their accelerating impact across society in a strategic and prioritized way, with present and future shifts in mind.

Disaster Recovery as a Service (DRaaS): third-party replication, hosting, and management of physical or virtual servers to provide switchover in the event of a disaster. This post outlines benefits of DRaaS.

Enterprise resource planning (ERP): the integrated management of core business processes, often in real-time and mediated by software and technology.

Ethernet: a network protocol that controls how data is transmitted over a LAN. Technically it is referred to as the IEEE 802.3 protocol. The protocol has evolved and improved over time and can now deliver at the speed of a gigabit per second.

Fast traffic switching: the ability to switch between voice sessions quickly in the event of a disruptive event. SDN devices need to be able to detect disruptive events and switch paths fast enough to maintain voice sessions. Click here for more about fast traffic switching, including details about how fast is fast enough.

Firewall: security feature that protects the VPN and terminating equipment from direct exposure to the Internet. This is one of the advantages of MPLS versus IP VPN over Internet.

Fourth Industrial Revolution (Industry Revolution 4.0): the current and developing environment in which disruptive technologies and trends such as the Internet of Things (IoT), robotics, virtual reality (VR), and artificial intelligence (AI) are changing the way we live and work.

Frame relay: a packet-switching telecommunication service designed for cost-efficient data transmission for intermittent traffic between local area networks (LANs) and between endpoints in wide area networks (WANs).

Gbps: short for Gigabits per second, a data transfer speed measurement for high-speed networks such as Gigabit Ethernet.

Health Insurance Portability and Accountability Act of 1996 (HIPAA): is United States legislation that provides data privacy and security provisions for safeguarding medical information.

Hybrid WAN: multiple connection types (e.g. MPLS circuits, carrier Ethernet, Internet, etc.) to deliver data to remote locations. Organizations use hybrid WANs to save money and significantly increase bandwidth.

International Ethernet private line (IEPL): a true Ethernet circuit from one end to the other, IEPL enables operation of the circuit without the need for a router or CSU/DSU because the circuit is configured on the MAC address level. The pure Ethernet circuit will provide less jitter and higher performance than the IPLC.

International private leased circuit (IPLC): functions as a point-to-point private line. IPLCs are usually TDM circuits that use Time Division Multiplexing to utilize the same circuit amongst many customers.

Internet protocol (IP): the method or protocol by which data is sent from one computer to another on the Internet. Each computer (known as a host) on the Internet has at least one IP address that uniquely identifies it from all other computers on the Internet.

Internet protocol security (IPsec): uses cryptographic security services to protect communications over Internet Protocol (IP) networks. *IPsec* supports network-level peer authentication, data-origin authentication, data integrity, data confidentiality (encryption), and replay protection.

Intrusion detection system (IDS) and intrusion prevention system (IPS): both increase the security level of networks, monitoring traffic and inspecting and scanning packets for suspicious data.

IP VPN: establishing seamless connectivity to a main network across an ISP. An IP VPN utilizes multiprotocol label switching

(MPLS) technology to prioritize Internet traffic and avoid public gateway to increase security, making it a layer 3 service.

Latency: the time lapse between when data is sent and when it is received, which can have a big impact on performance. Latency is an important consideration because some applications are particularly sensitive to latency. It's for these reasons that organizations typically run business class voice across MPLS It is important to also note that the degree of latency may also differ across carriers.

Local loop diversity: the use of more than one access loop that enters the customer facility from a diverse location. Best local loop diversity uses completely separate road paths to different central offices. When done correctly, can protect against disruption from failure (e.g., backhoe) in the physical link that connects the on-premise demarcation point to the telecommunications provider's network.

Jitter: measures delivery of packets in the proper order, which is of particular importance for VoIP. It is an important category for an MPLS Network Service Level Agreement.

Machine learning: a method of data analysis that automates analytical model building. It is a branch of artificial intelligence based on the idea that machines should be able to learn and adapt through experience.

Managed services provider (MSP): a service provider that delivers managed network services. May also be a CSP.

Mbps: means megabits per second. Mb is used in reference to download and upload speeds. It takes 8 bits of data to equal 1 byte.

MP BGP or multiprotocol BGP or multicast BGP: an extension to Border Gateway Protocol (BGP) that allows different types of addresses to be distributed in parallel. While standard BGP supports only IPv4 unicast addresses, Multiprotocol BGP supports IPv4 and IPv6 addresses and it supports unicast and multicast variants of each.

Multiprotocol label switching (MPLS): a type of data-carrying technique for high-performance telecommunications networks. *MPLS* directs data from one network node to the next based on short path labels rather than long network addresses, avoiding complex lookups in a routing table.

Network address translation (NAT): a method of remapping one IP address space into another by modifying network address information in IP header of packets while they are in transit across a traffic *routing* device.

Network blackout: refers to complete network outage and as the result network traffic stops.

Network brownout: refers to very poor performance of the network and as the result network traffic is in bad quality.

Network throughput: the rate of successful message delivery. Latency, packet loss, and WAN optimization can all impact throughput and network performance.

NFV: focuses on optimizing the network services themselves. NFV decouples the network functions, such as DNS, caching, etc., from proprietary hardware appliances, so they can run in software to accelerate service innovation and provisioning, particularly within service provider environments.

OpenDaylight (ODL): a modular open platform for customizing and automating networks of any size and scale. The *OpenDaylight* Project arose out of the SDN movement, with a clear focus on network programmability.

OpenFlow (OF): one of the first software-defined networking (SDN) standards. It originally defined the communication protocol in SDN environments that enables the SDN Controller to directly interact with the forwarding plane of network devices such as switches and routers, both physical and virtual (hypervisor-based), so it can better adapt to changing business requirements.

Optical carrier (OC) level: used to specify the speed of fiber optic networks conforming to the SONET standard. Click here for a list of speeds for common OC levels.

OSI model: the Open System Interconnection model defines a computer networking framework to implement protocols in seven layers. A protocol in the networking terms is a kind of negotiation and rule in between two networking entities.

Overlay network: a virtual network abstracted from the transport (underlay) network.

Packet loss: occurs when one or more packets is lost in transmission. Loss of packets can disrupt applications and/or cause errors. Lower packet losses and reduced latency are one of the reasons that organizations typically run business-class voice across MPLS services. Packet loss is an important SLA category for an MPLS Service Level Agreement.

Packet loss correction: a technical solution that can regenerate packets on the fly. Nevertheless, there are circumstances where packet loss correction may exacerbate the problem.

Payment card industry data security standard (PCI DSS): an information security standard for organizations that handle branded credit cards from the major card schemes. The *PCI* Standard is mandated by the card brands and administered by the Payment Card Industry Security Standards Council.

Peering: the voluntary connection of two separate networks so that they can exchange data for mutual benefit. Interconnecting MPLS networks requires subject matter expertise. Network professionals must understand MPLS internals, vendor-specific switch/router implementations, and carrier-specific COS markings.

Performance routing (PfR): balances loads, and dynamically picks the best route, to optimize bandwidth use and improve network availability. For these reasons, PfR is superior to BGP.

Policy-based routing (PBR): a technique used in computer networking to make routing decisions based on policies set by the network administrator… For example, a network administrator might want to forward a packet based on the source address, not the destination address.

Public Internet (public broadband Internet): a publicly accessible system of networks that connects computers around the world via the TCP/IP protocol.

Quality of Service (QoS): the level of service that results from applying Class of Service (CoS)—enables organizations to assign some types of traffic priority over others. There are several CoS treatments for MPLS networks.

Recovery point objective (RPO): the acceptable level of data loss measured in time (i.e., 5 minutes or 4 hours) in the event of a disaster. The amount of possible data loss, measured by either data or time, will help direct the Disaster Recovery/Business Continuity solution.

Recovery time objective (RTO): the amount of time it takes to get critical systems back into a functional state in the event of a disaster. The amount of time it takes to restore functionality will help direct the Disaster Recovery/Business Continuity solution.

Sales automation: an integrated application of customizable sales tools that can be used to automate and streamline the sales cycle. Sales automation functionality might include automated sales activities, forecasting, pipeline management, and tracking of customer interactions.

SDN: separates the network's control (brains) and forwarding (muscle) planes and provides a centralized view of the distributed network for more efficient orchestration and automation of network services.

SD-WAN controller: an SD-WAN function responsible for managing and controlling the SD-WAN Edges and SDWAN Gateways.

SD-WAN edge: the entity that provides all SD-WAN network functions (NFs) required where the SD-WAN overlay network (tunnel) is initiated and terminated. The NFs could be implemented as a physical CPE, a VNF running on a vCPE/uCPE, or a VNF running on a server in a data center. When referring to a particular implementation of this NF, you simply add an additional word indicating its implementation, e.g., SD-WAN Edge CPE, SD-WAN Edge VNF, etc.

SD-WAN edge CPE: the physical equipment implementation of an SD-WAN Edge.

SD-WAN edge VNF: the virtual network function (VNF) implementation of the SD-WAN Edge that can run on a vCPE/uCPE or server

SD-WAN gateway: an network function (physical or virtual) that provides interoperability between SD-WAN connections to other types of VPNs such as MPLS VPNs.

Service insertion: the ability to insert Layer 4 through Layer 7 software or hardware devices in the path of endpoints, easily facilitated by SD-WAN. These services can include, to name a few: firewalls, UTM, DDoS mitigation, and load balancing.

Service level agreement (SLA): a contract between an organization and a service provider that spells out the agreements between the two entities such as scope, quality, and responsibilities. The specific agreements depend upon what protections are most important to the organization. Categories for MPLS Service Level Agreements range from measures such as latency and packet loss to responsiveness of particular applications and satisfaction.

Session initiation protocol (SIP) trunking: enables elimination of expensive lower-speed voice and data lines by pooling them into one larger trunk. SIP trunking cost savings can be significant, as much as a 20% to 60% reduction as compared to traditional analog voice networks and packet switched data networks.

Simple network management protocol (SNMP): a popular protocol used for collecting information from and configuring network devices, such as servers, printers, hubs, switches, and routers on an Internet Protocol (IP) network.

Software as a Service (SaaS): a *software* distribution model in which a third-party provider hosts application and makes them available to customers over the Internet.

Software defined wide area network (SD-WAN): an approach to designing and deploying an enterprise wide area network (WAN) that uses software-defined networking (SDN) to determine the most effective way to route traffic to remote locations. SD-WAN can use multiple Internet circuits per location, as well as MPLS circuits.

Total cost of ownership (TCO): a financial estimate intended to help buyers and owners determine the direct and indirect costs of a product or system. It is a management accounting concept that can be used in full cost accounting or even ecological economics where it includes social costs.

Traffic shaping: technique which delays some packets to bring them into compliance with a desired *traffic profile.* Traffic shaping is used to optimize or guarantee performance for some kinds of packets by delaying other kinds. Traffic shaping prevents bandwidth-hungry applications from starving the voice sessions by allocating minimum and maximum amounts of bandwidth. VoIP and Video, for example, are typically given top and second priority over all other network traffic, in many networks.

Traffic steering: a technique to migrate application flows from one WAN link to another while preserving session persistency.

Transmission control protocol (TCP): is a protocol that defines how two hosts will establish a connection and exchange data. It guarantees that packets arrive in the order that they were sent.

Underlay network: the transport network over which the SD-WAN service operates. This could be an access network or core network.

Unified Communications as a Service (UCaaS): a category of "as a service" or "Cloud" delivery mechanisms for enterprise communications.

Unified threat management: an approach to security management that allows an administrator to monitor and manage a wide variety of security-related applications and infrastructure components through a single management console.

Virtual CPE (vCPE): a device located at the customer premises on which VNFs run using the Decentralized VNF deployment model defined in MEF's Carrier Ethernet and NFV paper. Note that vCPE, uCPE, and "white box" servers are often used interchangeably in the industry.

Virtual private LAN service (VPLS): is a technology that provides Ethernet-based multipoint communication over IP/MPLS networks. It allows geographically dispersed sites to share an Ethernet broadcast domain by connecting sites through pseudo-wires. There are advantages and disadvantages to VPLS.

Virtual private network (VPN): a method of linking two or more locations on a public network as if they are on a private network. This post describes the pros and cons of IP VPN over Internet vs. MPLS.

Voice over Internet protocol (VoIP): a technology that allows you to make voice calls using a broadband Internet connection instead of a regular (or analog) phone line.

VPN backup: included with IP VPN over Internet, enables switchover to another Internet circuit in the event that the primary connection fails so that users can keep working. This is one of the advantages of IP VPN over Internet versus MPLS.

VPN tunnel: is a secure path between two locations through the Internet, secured by the use of encryption.

VRF identifier: Virtual Routing and Forwarding identifiers allow multiple isolated routing tables to exist on a single routing system. VRFs can permit path isolation on a network.

WAN acceleration: increases the speed of access to applications and information. WAN acceleration is also known as WAN optimization. The Cloud may kill WAN optimization as more data flows through the Internet to the Cloud, rather than traveling directly between two points.

WAN optimization: increases the speed of access to applications and information. WAN optimization is also known as WAN acceleration. The Cloud may kill WAN optimization as more data flows through the Internet to the Cloud, rather than traveling directly between two points. WAN Optimization Methods for improving performance over a WAN which can include data compression, TCP re-transmission optimizations (optimized for low bandwidth & high latency networks), application proxies, data de-duplication, forward error correction, etc.

Zero touch provisioning (ZTP): a switch feature that allows the devices to be provisioned and configured automatically, eliminating most of the manual labor involved with adding them to a network.

About the Author

David W. Wang is the managing principal, industry evangelist, and senior consultant for ITCom Global, LLC, based in Washington, DC metro. David has been the director and senior manager of strategic business development for both startup and Fortune 20 telecom/IT companies in the US and global marketplace. He is also the author of the book *Cash in on Cloud Computing* (2015). Business contact email: ITComG18@gmail.com.

Index

N

O

P

Q

Milton Keynes UK
Ingram Content Group UK Ltd.
UKHW040051071024
449327UK00019B/481

9 780367 570835